Young Millionaires

Young Millionaires

Inspiring Stories To Ignite Your Entrepreneurial Dreams

By Rieva Lesonsky,
Editorial Director, *Entrepreneur* Magazine,
and Gayle Sato Stodder

Entrepreneur Media Inc.
2392 Morse Ave., Irvine, CA 92614

Current titles from Entrepreneur Media Inc.:
Start Your Own Business: The Only Start-up Book You'll Ever Need

Forthcoming titles from Entrepreneur Media Inc.:
303 Marketing Ideas Guaranteed to Boost Your Business
Business Plans Made Easy: It's Not as Hard (or as Boring) as You Think
Where's The Money? Financing Solutions for Your Small Business
Knockout Marketing: Powerful Secrets to Punch Up Your Sales

Managing Editor: Marla Markman
Copy Editor: Marie B. Morris
Proofreader: Marisa Laudadio
Production Design: Coghill Composition Company
Cover Design: Janice Olson & Associates

This publication is designed to provide accurate and authoritative information
in regard to the subject matter covered. It is sold with the understanding that
the publisher is not engaged in rendering legal, accounting or other professional services. If legal advice or other expert assistance is required, the services of
a competent professional person should be sought.

Library of Congress Cataloging-in-Publication Data
Lesonsky, Rieva.
    Entrepreneur magazine's young millionaires : inspiring
stories to ignite your entrepreneurial dreams / by Rieva Lesonsky
and Gayle Sato Stodder.
    p.   cm.
    ISBN 1-891984-01-2
    1. New business enterprises—United States—Case studies.
2. Entrepreneurship—United States—Case studies.   3. Success in
business—United States—Case studies.   4. Millionaires—United
States—Case studies.   I. Stodder, Gayle Sato.
II. Entrepreneur Media Inc. (Irvine, Calif.)   III. Title.
    HD62.5.L466   1998   98–27541
    338'.04'0973—dc21   CIP

Printed in the United States of America

08 07 06 05 04 03 02 01 00 99   10 9 8 7 6 5 4 3 2

To the entrepreneurs
who inspire us every day.
—*RIEVA LESONSKY*

To my self-made dad,
who set the standard.
—*GAYLE SATO STODDER*

Acknowledgments

Without the daily brilliance of the *Entrepreneur* editorial staff, this book would not have been possible. Special thanks to books managing editor Marla Markman for her diligence, patience and advocacy. Appreciation also goes out to Gayle Sato Stodder, whose hard work, dedication and brilliance helped transform these entrepreneurial stories into inspiration for us all. Thanks also to the *Entrepreneur* writers whose original works formed the basis for this book: Lynn Beresford, Janean Chun, Connie Cousins, G. David Doran, Holly Celeste Fisk, Cynthia E. Griffin, Frances Huffman, Erika Kotite, Charlotte Mulhern, Heather Page, Debra Phillips, Karen E. Spaeder, Guen Sublette, Karen Sulkis and Elaine W. Teague. And thanks to Susan Stone Russell, who was the backbone for this project, and to the Marias (Anton and Valdez), who help me do my best every day.

—*Rieva Lesonsky*

My contribution to this book was a whole-family effort. For his unflagging support in this and all other impossible endeavors, Matthew Stodder deserves more gratitude than words can express. If not for the priceless help and friendship of Claudia Marquecho, none of this would have made it to print. Thanks to Hana Stodder, who reminded me every night "Mommy, you can do it!" and to my entrepreneurial mom, Elaine Sato, whose example is a continual inspiration.

Finally, to the entrepreneurs whose stories breathe life into the pages that follow, thank you for your openness, for indulging our curiosity, for sharing your hard-earned secrets and for offering unconditional encouragement. Your generosity enriches us all.

—*Gayle Sato Stodder*

Table of Contents

Introduction

Table of Contents

Table of Contents

Chapter 4: Break The Rules

Table of Contents

CHAPTER 5: If This Were My Company . . .

Table of Contents

Table of Contents

Table of Contents

Table of Contents

Introduction

*"Whatever you can do
or dream you can,
begin it. Boldness has genius,
power and magic in it.
Begin it now."*
—Goethe

This is a book that invites you to believe. Look elsewhere for details on writing a business plan or setting up your accounting system. If you want statistics to help you divine your probability of success, consult your local reference librarian. This book isn't about mechanics.

And it isn't about common sense.

In the pages that follow, you'll meet 101 entrepreneurs aged 40 and younger whose companies have reached the magic million-dollar mark—and beyond. They've taken many roads to get there. Some struck it rich before they got their bearings; others hammered away at one idea after another until they finally hit gold. Some had sophisticated backgrounds in finance and sales; others began while still in high school. There are dreamers, pragmatists, wanderers, tinkerers and innovators. Some were born to the task of building a business; others learned by trial and error.

They all have one thing in common: At some point in their lives, they stepped out of their familiar worlds and into the unknown. This book is about taking that step, and about the adventures that inevitably follow.

What emerges is a vision of what's possible in life. It begins with Mark Beckloff and Dan Dye cutting out dog biscuits at the kitchen table, follows Amy Scherber through France in pursuit of the perfect bread, drops in on Dave Kapell erecting "poetry walls" to celebrate the success of his Magnetic Poetry kits, sits down with Bill and Gina Ellis as they contemplate the next move for their slipcovered furniture business, and closes the day at John and Tracy Porter's Stonehouse Farm, where entrepreneurship and the well-lived life twine together like morning glory vines.

We chose to focus on young entrepreneurs for a variety of reasons. Perhaps most important was this: They embody the boldest entrepreneurship has to offer. These people didn't wait until they had acquired a full complement of business skills, or until they had millions at their disposal. They simply acted.

Often, their acts were irrational. A 17-year-old at the helm of her own clothing company? A 14-year-old pioneering Internet services in his hometown? A 24-year-old Alaskan commercial fisherman designing hats? You probably wouldn't have bet on any of them at the beginning of their careers.

That would be your loss. Today, Jennifer Barclay's Blue Fish Clothing Co. sells nearly $14 million worth of artisan-crafted apparel annually, ExchangeNet co-founder Michael Krause's Internet service company grosses over $1 million, and ex-fisherman Barry Barr's hats are among the many innovative outdoor products that contribute to Kavu's $3 million in sales.

Outrageous? Exactly. Here is living proof that the impossible happens—every day, to ordinary people.

Yet this is not a book of fairy tales. No magic spells or fairy godmothers take the place of hard work and daring. The entrepreneurs in this book have succeeded by doing more than they ever dreamed they could—by working harder and for longer hours, by mustering talents they never knew they had, by making personal sacrifices they didn't think they were capable of, and by conjuring a faith so powerful that even the most overwhelming obstacles were simply no match. In the end, these folks tapped into a force much more formidable than magic. It's not just that their accomplishments outstrip those of the average twenty- or thirtysomething. It's that they've attained a level of self-determination most people never know. In an era when job security and lifetime careers are a thing of the past, nothing could be more empowering. Their experience hasn't turned them into egomaniacs, though; it's given them humility.

"Everybody should be required to do two things in life," says publisher and entrepreneur Mike Freihofer. "One is waiting tables, and the other is starting a business. Those two things will give you a perspective on life that you can't get anywhere else."

Freihofer and the others in this book have a common message for would-be entrepreneurs: Do it now. Don't wait. Entrepreneurship demands more than you imagine possible, but the human spirit is never mightier than when it's tested. You don't have to be seasoned or wealthy or connected—or sane. Whether you know it or not, you already have everything you need.

Chapter 1

Let Opportunity Find You

"The world is full of magical things patiently waiting for our wits to grow sharper."

—BERTRAND RUSSELL

Dan Dye, 39
Mark Beckloff, 34

Three Dog Bakery

WHAT THEY DO: Operate upscale bakeries for dogs; manufacture wholesale gourmet dog treats; produce mail order "dogalog"
HOME BASE: Kansas City, Missouri
FOUNDED: 1990
START-UP COSTS: $1,000
1997 SALES: $3 million
1998 PROJECTIONS: $10 million

Photo© Steven Curtis

The bone-shaped cookie cutter tucked into Mark Beckloff's Christmas stocking was supposed to be a joke—a mom's way of teasing her son about his slavish devotion to dogs. Beckloff took the joke, then used it to make a batch of bone-shaped dog cookies.

They were good enough to eat. So good, in fact, that Beckloff began to wonder whether he wasn't onto something. If his dogs, Sarah, Gracie and Dottie, found the cookies irresistible, wouldn't others? And wouldn't the same foodies who shelled out $10 a pound for gourmet coffee pay an extra few bucks for good-tasting dog biscuits?

Dogged Determination

"We had lots of interest [from the beginning], but it was a rough ride. We were doubling sales each year, and that's hard to sustain. We almost lost our house twice, and I can distinctly remember times when I had to take cash advances on my Visa to make payroll. But we never quit believing it would work. Never did we consider giving up. It gets to a point where you figure 'We have everything into this, so we've got to keep going.' And you do."

—MARK BECKLOFF

Beckloff and his soon-to-be business partner Dan Dye were intrigued enough to convert the kitchen table into a makeshift production line. "At first, we wholesaled to health-food stores and vets' offices," says Beckloff. "We got such positive reviews, we kept going."

In time, the side venture became a full-time business, allowing Beckloff and Dye to quit their corporate jobs and become bakers. When the business outgrew their home, the partners found a commercial space that became the base for their manufacturing operations. "Then, we figured, since we were there baking anyway, we might as well open our doors to [retail] customers," says Beckloff. "We paid $50 for a used bakery case and started selling our cookies to the public."

Success has dogged them ever since. Then called KC-K9, the world's first gourmet dog bakery was an instant hit with pampered pups and their doting parents. From the beginning, the pupcakes, Scotty biscotti, Great Danish and collie-flowers sold like hotcakes.

Dye and Beckloff are admittedly suckers for a good pun, but it's not just clever merchandising that makes their bakery a success. They genuinely love dogs. They're as committed to healthful, high-quality products as they are to mirthful marketing; their treats are made without preservatives, sodium, sugar or fillers. And they don't begrudge their loyal customers a free sample or two.

"Dogs are always jumping up into the barrels and helping themselves to a bone," Dye says philosophically. "But we can't prosecute them because the handcuffs would slip off their paws."

Besides, who's to complain about a clientele that supports a nationwide network of wholesale accounts, a mail order "dogalog," and nine retail locations? In 1998, Dye and Beckloff hope to add even more outlets through licensing agreements. Thanks to a nation of discriminating dogs, Beckloff and Dye are the authors of a cookbook memoir, *Short Tails and Treats from the Three Dog Bakery*, and hosts of the TV Food Network show. They're also hopelessly devoted to Three Dog's "founding sisters"—a black Labrador named Sarah; Gracie, a Great Dane; and Dalmatian Dottie—whose initial enthusiasm helped turn a gag gift into a growing business. "What we've given people is a way to celebrate their dogs' lives," says Beckloff. "That's the whole message here. One of the coolest things that's come out of this experience is that [the dogs] have fans all over the world. People write them letters and send them everything for Christmas."

Everything, perhaps, except bone-shaped cookie cutters. Dye and Beckloff have the cookies covered.

Photo© Dale Berman

David Leib, 32
Caren Schlom, 31

Siany Bag Co.

WHAT THEY DO: Manufacture and retail leather handbags, tote bags and luggage

HOME BASE: Woodland Hills, California

FOUNDED: 1992

START-UP COSTS: $5,000

1997 SALES: $1.3 million

1998 PROJECTIONS: $2.2 million

Like plenty of other American tourists, Caren Schlom and David Leib were thrilled to discover that leather tote bags in Greece sold for a song—for about one-fourth of what folks would pay in the States. And so, like millions of travelers before them, Schlom and Leib bought two bags as souvenirs and returned home to a shower of compliments.

Bag The Job

"When we started the business, I was basically a bag peddler [at college fairs]. It was 'Here's the bag; here's the money. Thank you.' Now, I'm doing the buying, handling personnel, overseeing a 15-person staff. Every year I say I'm going to leave the business [and go back to the entertainment industry]. But I don't think I'd have had the opportunities to do as much there as I have in my own company."

—CAREN SCHLOM

But unlike most tourists, Leib and Schlom didn't stop there. They decided to try turning a profit by importing the bags and selling them at college fairs and craft shows. "We both had full-time jobs," Schlom recalls. Leib was a mortgage banker; Schlom worked for Fox Television. "But we knew this was a product that [could be] geared toward college students, and the investment we needed to open a booth was relatively low." If the venture turned into a lucrative sideline, the partners reasoned, they'd be satisfied.

Before they knew it, Leib had quit his job, maxed out his credit cards, and begun selling the bags in earnest on the college fair circuit. "One week, we did $10,000 in sales," says Schlom. That was enough to convince Schlom to quit her job as well. Siany (named after the Italian town Schlom once bought a leather tote bag in) has been the partners' full-time bag ever since.

In the six years they've been in business, Leib and Schlom have transformed their apartment-based "road show" into a more serious operation, complete with four retail locations and a product line that includes name-brand briefcases, handbags, belts and shoes. They've also solidified their partnership—on the personal side by getting married, and professionally by dividing responsibilities so that the company can take advantage of Leib's financial savvy and Schlom's people skills.

Although starting young has had its challenges—"Every day has been a learning experience," Schlom says—it has had advantages as well. "If we had known what was involved in running a company like this when we started, we never would have done it. You have to do it when you have nothing to lose."

G. Dana Sinkler Jr., 38
Alexander Dzieduszycki, 39
Terra Chips

WHAT THEY DO: Make snack chips from
    gourmet potatoes, taro root,
    sweet potatoes and yucca

HOME BASE: Brooklyn, New York

FOUNDED: 1990

START-UP COSTS: $50,000 to $60,000

1997 SALES: Over $15 million

1998 PROJECTIONS: $18 million to
    $20 million

Photo© *Crain's New York Business/*Sherri Nickol

8

Alexander Dzieduszycki and Dana Sinkler were a couple of hard-working caterers looking for a trademark. "On the bar at every party in New York City, you'd see an elaborate platter of *crudités*," recalls Sinkler. "We thought we'd do something different—a signature dish that would tell everyone it was a Dana Alexander party."

Chips Off The Same Block

"I think our partnership works because Alex and I are both hard-working. We strive for perfection. We don't have to wonder whether the other is doing his job."

—DANA SINKLER

They decided on chips. Not run-of-the-mill potato chips, mind you, but crisp, flavorful chips made from exotic taro, sweet potatoes and yucca. Folks gobbled them with such alacrity that the partners began to suspect that the newfound snacks would be just as addictive on retail shelves.

Then came the moment of truth. "We went to Saks Fifth Avenue [a former catering client] about three weeks after we made the vegetable chips," Dzieduszycki recalls. "They were packaged for food service in a utilitarian foil bag with a black-and-white label. As we were explaining to the public relations person how we were going to come out with new packaging for retailers, she said, 'I want it in the store right now!'"

The partners were happy to oblige, and a business was born. Terra Chips had the same appeal as a retail product that it did at New York's trendiest parties: People couldn't stop munching them. That was a good thing, says Sinkler, because runaway growth kept the partners on their feet. "Thank God we had a product that was driven by demand," he observes, "because we were spending all of our time trying to figure out how to pay the bills."

The answer to their monetary prayers came in 1995

when an investment group agreed to acquire Terra Chips—and keep the partners in place at the helm of the company. In turn, one of that investment group's holdings, Arrowhead Mills, acquired Terra Chips in 1997.

Becoming part of a larger organization—with a larger capital pool—has meant the difference between being a real player in the snack food universe and being just another flash in the pan, Sinkler says. Sales are on the rise, a new line of Yukon Gold potato chips has won an impressive following, and the company is running at peak performance.

"When I take a step back, it's a pretty awesome thing," says Sinkler. "Seven years ago, we were frying chips at home in a wok. Now, we're selling $15 million worth of product a year. We've learned a hell of a lot."

Peter Kim, 39

Yummy Management Co.

WHAT THEY DO: Run 19 food-service locations, including Yummy Korean Barbecue, Bear's Kitchen, Chow Mein Express, Taco King and an assortment of franchise operations

HOME BASE: Honolulu

FOUNDED: 1987

START-UP COSTS: $75,000

1997 SALES: About $10 million

1998 PROJECTIONS: Not available

As a kicker for the University of Alabama and the Tampa Bay Buccaneers, Peter Kim took plenty of hard knocks. When he suffered an injury early in his professional football career, he was sidelined permanently.

That was how Kim ended up back in his native Honolulu with the idea of becoming a G-man. "I had applied for jobs with the ATF and the FBI," he recalls. "I had passed their tests, but I had to wait a year before they would [make an assignment]."

Run With It

"My college football coach, [Bear] Bryant, said, 'You can do anything you set your mind to.' But he also said, 'You have to be sensible about what you're good at.' [Aspiring entrepreneurs] need to evaluate themselves in an accurate way. They need to ask themselves, 'What am I good for? What can I do?' I can never be a rocket scientist, I tell you that. But I have been able to run this business."

While he was waiting, Kim agreed to help his sister, Jeannie Choi, open a Korean barbecue restaurant. It would be an amusement, a good deed. "That restaurant [the original Yummy Korean Barbecue] did 300 percent better than we projected," he recalls. "Next thing I knew, I had opened five locations in a year," including a spot at Honolulu's wildly popular Ala Moana shopping center.

"The day we opened at Ala Moana, the ATF called me," Kim says. "I politely asked for 90 days to think about it, but obviously I never went in that direction."

The government's loss was the food world's gain. Though he had no specific food-service experience, Kim quickly formulated a winning game plan: Serve high-quality, regionally appealing food to a convenience-hungry market. "This term doesn't exist in the food industry, but we categorize ourselves as 'semifast food,' " explains Kim. "We're serving restaurant-quality food at a fast-food price and a fast-food pace."

Over the years, Kim has applied this philosophy to a varied menu of operations. He's behind a string of Yummy Korean Barbecue locations, upscale plate-lunch restaurants called Bear's Kitchen (named after Kim's college football coach, Bear Bryant), and a host of Mexican, Chinese, ice cream, pizza, and chicken joints (some franchised, some not). In addition to Yummy Management's 19 locations, Kim's family members run another 12 food-service businesses.

All told, Kim's little detour into food service hasn't been a bad day's work. "This is a tough business," he reflects. "The work is nonstop. It's seven days a week, and the holidays are the busiest time of year. But it's rewarding to see the business grow."

Ray Barnes, 36
Louise Barnes, 35
Crime Scene Clean-up

WHAT THEY DO: Clean up scenes of homicides, suicides and accidents; four locations, in Maryland, Georgia, Pennsylvania and South Carolina

HOME BASE: Fallston, Maryland

FOUNDED: 1993

START-UP COSTS: Less than $10,000

1997 SALES: Over $3 million

1998 PROJECTIONS: Not available

Photo© *People Weekly*/Vickie Lewis

No one wants to do what Ray and Louise Barnes do—not even Ray and Louise Barnes. But without their service, scores of families already shocked by tragedies would have to endure the secondary horror of cleaning up the aftermath.

Ray knows firsthand how difficult that can be. "My grandfather shot himself, and I cleaned it up," he recalls. "It was awful. But, obviously, I didn't want my mother or my grandmother being traumatized by that."

That was when Ray was 22. He went on to a career as a forensic investigator for the Baltimore medical examiner's office, where he came face to face with the need for a specialized cleaning service for survivors of trauma. "I got a lot of calls there from people who needed help," says Ray. "There was no one available who was properly trained to do this kind of work."

Commitment On Call

"This business is our baby. No one else is going to have the heart-and-soul drive that we do. It's difficult being on call all the time, but until we are comfortable having someone else run things, we'll be there."

—RAY BARNES

Cleaning up after a trauma is not the same as routine house cleaning. Ray has developed a proprietary cleaning solution to tackle the job. And he makes sure that the medical waste is disposed of safely and legally.

There's a human component as well. "You don't run this kind of business; it runs you," Ray says. "When a family member calls, you go. Too bad if you've only had an hour's sleep or you just sat down to a five-star meal. Louise and I have gone out on Christmas Day. These people can't wait for a convenient time; you can't ask them to wait. They need fast service."

On the other hand, if ever a business was necessary and appreciated, this is it. In addition to the financial rewards, Louise and Ray are gratified to offer some solace to people who so clearly need it. "I don't enjoy doing this," says Ray, "but I enjoy saving families from having to do it themselves."

Kerry Townsend, 34

Timely Temporaries

WHAT THEY DO: Secretarial and light industrial job placement; three locations

HOME BASE: Minneapolis

FOUNDED: 1994

START-UP COSTS: $50,000

1997 SALES: $3.5 million

1998 PROJECTIONS: $4.2 million

If Kerry Townsend had been running five minutes late, he might never have started his own business. But as things turned out, Townsend—a recruiter for a temporary help firm—ran into an old client one day and started to chat. "We'd always had a good relationship," says Townsend. "As we got to talking, he asked me if I'd be interested in staffing his plant."

Townsend hadn't thought much about striking out on his own. He had a stable career and wasn't particularly unhappy with his job. But in that moment, he began to think about becoming an entrepreneur. He had a substantial client ready to sign on. He had talent, energy and intelligence.

The next thing he knew, Townsend was in business.

By The Rules

"One of the most difficult things about running this business is trying to comply with all the government regulations. You have to be on the lookout at all times, and even then you find out after the fact about new regulations [that apply to you because you've reached a certain number of employees]."

"I basically started the business at [the client's plant]," says Townsend. "I maintained an office at home, and I used it to get additional business off the ground. But I did all the interviews at the plant, all the human resources introductory programs there. Most companies start from an empty office and try like anything to get their first clients. I had a major leg up."

Of course, Townsend had some facility for the business. By the end of his first year, he had 450 employees on his roster; today, he has more than 2,100.

True, Townsend got into the business during a temporary help boom. "A majority of our growth is due to growth in the economy," he says. But a booming industry has its downsides as well. For one thing, there's competition. And, Townsend adds, "Now, metropolitan Minneapolis has one of the lowest unemployment rates in the country. We've been fortunate to have a format of active recruiting over the years, which is compatible with a tight labor market. We're used to selling an applicant on a job; it's been the key to our growth."

Townsend admits that entrepreneurship is a bit more strenuous than being an employee. "There's no such thing as a 40-hour workweek," he says. "I've got employees working 24 hours a day, seven days a week. I have to be available to handle problems when they arise."

But he also enjoys the satisfaction of having built a thriving business from little more than a chance encounter. His advice to other young people with entrepreneurial aspirations: "Take every chance that you can to do it on your own. Don't let anyone tell you it can't be done."

Jimmy Jones, 34

Lady Fairway Golf Shoes Inc.

WHAT THEY DO: Manufacture women's golf shoes and accessories
HOME BASE: Tampa, Florida
FOUNDED: 1993
START-UP COSTS: $200,000
1997 SALES: $4.4 million
1998 PROJECTIONS: $5 million

Photo© Chris Coxwell

Jimmy Jones was there as a husband. His wife, pro golfer Dawn Coe-Jones, was on tour, and Jones was with her to be supportive. Sympathetic. Nice. What did all this sympathetic niceness get him? An earful of complaints about women's golf shoes.

"The women on the tour knew I had [sold] shoes at Converse, and they always told me how badly their golf shoes fit," says Jones, who had been a sales executive there. Initially, he may have found the topic wearing—until he realized the inspiration it contained.

"I saw that [women's golf shoes] were something that an undercapitalized guy like me could get into," says Jones. "I couldn't have gotten into clubs. I couldn't have gotten into balls or men's shoes; those were all dominated by big companies. But none of the big boys were looking at women's shoes [seriously]. The timing was perfect."

Avoid The Traps

"We've been lucky never to have been face to face with failure, but failure is a motivator that never goes away. Any [entrepreneur] who tells you that failure isn't an issue is fooling you—and probably fooling themselves."

Indeed. Five months after Jones' Lady Fairway Golf Shoes hit the market in 1993, the company turned a profit. The secret? Instead of using scaled-down men's shoes, Jones designed shoes to fit women's feet. He also recognized that women cared about style and price as much as they did about fit and comfort. Though pro shops were skeptical at first, women golfers got it immediately. By 1994, Jones' second year in business, Lady Fairway was already grossing $2.2 million.

Exhilarating as it was to launch a breakthrough—and breakaway—product, Jones recalls his first year in business as a bit of a sprint. "I did my first $1 million in sales with just myself and one employee," he says. "All we had was a word processor—no computers. I kept inventory by pencil." For a guy who just months earlier had been COO of an international sporting goods company, the change was bracing. "It was crazy," Jones says with a laugh. "I don't know how we did it."

And of course, that was only the opening drive. Since then, Jones has faced increasing competition from major corporations. "Suddenly, the giants of the men's shoe business have started paying attention to this market," he says. While it's scary going toe to toe with big companies, so far Jones is still in the game. "Women like products that are made for women," he says. "We're holding our own."

The next round of challenges: Expanding the Lady Fairway brand name beyond the world of shoes. "We've already branched out into gloves, socks, hats and visors. Next, we'll be coming out with accessories," Jones reports.

But he is not relying solely on new products to grow the company. He's also deploying the same high level of customer service that has helped put Lady Fairway on the map. "If [a retailer] buys a pair of our shoes and there's a problem, they can send them back. The same is true for the end user; if they don't like the shoes, they can return them," says Jones. "I have to make it easy for customers to do business with us, and [the difference] has to be big in order to separate us from the giants."

In other words, Jones is listening—not just because listening is germane to the health of his business, but *just in case*. The seeds of opportunity are everywhere, even on the golf course, even when you aren't the one golfing. Somewhere, amid all those complaints about aching feet, might be the sole of a business.

Chapter 2

Believe

> "All you need
> in this life
> are ignorance
> and confidence,
> and then
> success is sure."
>
> —MARK TWAIN

Robin Petgrave, 36

Bravo Helicopters & Wings

WHAT THEY DO: Helicopter and airplane
    flight training, tours and trans-
    portation; car rentals
HOME BASE: Torrance, California
FOUNDED: 1991
START-UP COSTS: $450
1997 SALES: $2.5 million
1998 PROJECTIONS: $3.7 million

Even if Robin Petgrave never went near a helicopter, he'd be airborne. We're not just talking about his vocation; it's his personality. So energetic is Petgrave that the mental picture of him flying around—with or without a helicopter—is pretty much unavoidable.

Exuberance comes in handy when you're trying to launch a helicopter training school on $300—and you don't own a helicopter. "I remember that the business license cost $450," says Petgrave. That made the $300 bank balance even more of a handicap. Yet modest funds didn't stop Petgrave, who got his company off the ground by persuading a helicopter leasing firm to rent to him without the usual $6,000 security deposit.

Lofty Ideals

"It's much simpler to be honest and treat people well. This way, if someone calls me up and says I tried to cheat them seven years ago, I don't have to think about it or remember the exact conversation; I know that isn't how I do business. I don't like having to keep up with my own lies."

"I said to them, 'If you let me lease the helicopter, I'll pay a higher rate because I don't have the security deposit,'" Petgrave recalls. "They said, 'Why should we do that?' And I said, 'Because your helicopter's just sitting here now, and it's not making you any money.'" They got the point.

"You don't have to have money to make money," Petgrave insists. "As long as you have something that people want, you can get them to pay for it. If you offer a prepayment discount, you can use the [cash] to get what you need. Then it just becomes a cash flow juggling act."

Of course, that assumes you can inspire people to want what you have to sell. Here, Petgrave has two major advantages. First is the inevitable thrill of flying, which doesn't require much advertisement. And second is his obvious enthusiasm for being up in the air. "If I wasn't flying for a living, I'd be saving all my money to do it on my own time," he quips. "I'm not really a businessman; I'm a pilot who's working as a businessman so I can keep my job."

And running a $2.5 million company is a job. Chief among Petgrave's challenges: "Damn employees." Though his affection for his staff is apparent, Petgrave notes that keeping employees informed, motivated and on track is an ongoing project. "As the business grows, you're trying to duplicate yourself," he says. "That's hard [in a variety of ways.] For example, you make mistakes, but you catch them right away. When an employee makes a mistake, you might not find out about it for a long time. Catching other people's mistakes is harder."

Also, adds Petgrave, "I never used to understand what people meant when they said you have to be a people person to manage employees. I thought, 'Why? You just tell them what they're supposed to do.' But it's not that simple. You have to be able to maneuver people to do what's going to benefit them—and benefit you."

On the other hand, Petgrave openly acknowledges that his staff is responsible for his success. "I'm not that smart, but I've surrounded myself with smart, highly motivated people," he says. "Recently, I was sitting down with some business associates who were making me go through the painful process of making decisions, which I hate. And they were saying, 'You know, you made some good decisions here today.' Five years ago, I would have had no clue what to do in these situations. But because I've had the benefit of working with smart people over the years, I can make good decisions myself now."

Which is not to say that Petgrave has gone sensible. However stable, established and respected his business is, it's not about staying the course. His is a company built on winging it.

"If you're scared, you're too cautious and you aren't going to get as far," Petgrave asserts. "At any time, the right set of occurrences could cause me to lose everything. But you can't think like that. You prepare for the worst, but you have the intention of doing well."

Sharon Fisher, 40

Memories Unlimited Inc.

WHAT THEY DO: Special events and recreational consulting

HOME BASE: Orlando, Florida

FOUNDED: 1992

START-UP COSTS: $3,000

1997 SALES: $1 million

1998 PROJECTIONS: $1.3 million

Photo© Gary Bernloehr

If you see Sharon Fisher wearing a giant crab costume or building a race car out of vegetables, you can assume she's hard at work. No, Fisher isn't undergoing some strange form of therapy. She's pioneering a new industry that revolves around the notion of "play with a purpose"—and, happily for Fisher and her staff, also for a profit.

Fisher's company, Memories Unlimited, coordinates "participatory events" for corporate meetings, conventions, promotions and similar gatherings. What does that mean in practical terms? "For the morning break at a corporate seminar, we might plan a game show that incorporates information people learned [in the classroom]," Fisher explains. Other possibilities include island treks, treasure hunts, cardboard boat regattas, video scavenger hunts, and wacky olympics.

All In A Day's Fun

"You need to do what you're good at and what you love. When you do, the opportunities before you become crystal clear and you know what to do. It becomes easy to be successful."

All this is pure vindication for Fisher, who faced her share of skepticism when she decided to pursue a major in recreation. After earning her degree, she worked as a consultant for a city recreation department, then for an upscale resort. It was there, planning events for the resort's corporate clients, that Fisher first saw an opportunity to make fun into a serious business.

In fact, it's the very concept of "serious business" that makes Fisher's service so vital. "In their drive for profits and productivity, companies sometimes miss the boat [when it comes to] adding fun," she says. "Plato said, 'You can learn more about a person in an hour of play than in a year of conversation.'"

Yet the average manager is better equipped to deliver a

six-hour lecture on fire safety procedures than to orchestrate a collegiate brainpower contest. "Here, we're all recreation professionals," says Fisher. "When we put an event together, everyone participates. Everyone is safe. The timing is right. Everything works the way it's supposed to."

Sound easy? It's not. But it is fun—and that's reward enough for Fisher. "When we say our mission is 'play with a purpose,' we really believe that work should be fun," Fisher says. "Almost everyone who works with me gave up a great job and took a pay cut to work here because they believe in what we're doing.

"I could never work at a customer complaints desk," muses Fisher. "I have the skills to do it, but I'd just hate that job. All of our clients are in the market for fun, so we're always working with people who are in a good mood. That in itself is a kind of reward."

Kermit Heartsong, 38

Quantum Gameworks

WHAT THEY DO: Publish 42 educational
and strategy games

HOME BASE: San Francisco

FOUNDED: 1990

START-UP COSTS: $40,000

1997 SALES: Over $1 million

1998 PROJECTIONS: $3.8 million

Kermit Heartsong is an engineer by training, "but I knew I didn't want to be an engineer," he says. "So after I got my degree, I immediately began working in other fields." He set tile, cleaned garages, hung Sheetrock. And he looked for ways to help the community, volunteering to work with kids who were at risk.

Better Gamesmanship

"When you're trying to launch something, there's nothing more important than research, research, research. I called and bugged the guys who developed Trivial Pursuit for six months until they decided to fly me out to talk with them."

It was there that inspiration struck. "In these neighborhoods, you'd see kids whose parents took an active role in their education and kids whose families were not involved, and the difference was overwhelming," says Heartsong. "The common link [among the families who were involved] was reading and playing games within the family. I saw an opportunity to create games that parents and children could play together without the child being intimidated or the parent being bored."

Already interested in games, Heartsong had invented a word game to improve his own vocabulary after college. He knew he could create quality "edu-tainment." The next challenge was raising money.

"It was very difficult to raise capital," Heartsong reports. "I'm an African-American, which made it even more difficult. But we were already getting wonderful reviews on our games. And with perseverance, we were finally able to find investors who understood what we were doing and believed in it."

Today, Quantum's games are available at specialty retail outlets throughout the United States and Canada, including FAO Schwarz, The Nature Company and Zany Brainy. International expansion is in the works, and so is a mail order venture.

Why are Quantum's games so successful? Says Heartsong: "They're products that impart something. We spend a lot of time perfecting the play structure. These aren't [heavily hyped] toys that kids play with for a few days and then forget about. They're quality products."

On another level, Heartsong has tapped into the same concern that first prompted him to volunteer as a tutor all those years ago. "There's a segment of parents who understand the value of playing games with their kids, because that's what they had growing up," he says. "They're interested in reaching back and recapturing that experience."

Amy Scherber, 38

Amy's Bread

WHAT THEY DO: Make fabulous bread;
sell it at two retail locations and to
30 wholesale accounts

HOME BASE: New York City

FOUNDED: 1992

START-UP COSTS: $150,000

1997 SALES: Over $2 million

1998 PROJECTIONS: $3 million

Photo Courtesy: Amy's Bread

Not so long ago, the best thing since sliced bread was—well, sliced bread. Bread had become a production-line item, something to be cranked out and mass-produced. Luckily for the bread eaters of the world, chef Amy Scherber looked at the lowly loaf and saw potential.

Her decision came partly by default. "I had worked as a chef in all parts of the kitchen [during the '80s]," Scherber explains. "I enjoyed baking, but I didn't want to work with sugar all day. I'd often end up feeling sick from tasting all those sweets." Bread was easier on Scherber's metabolism and—not incidentally—was a daily thing. "Everybody loves good bread," Scherber observes. "At that time, bread was not a big thing in New York, but I had a gut feeling about it. I really thought bread was going to be a big trend."

What's Kneaded

"People look at this business and think the profits must be very high because all you're selling is flour and water. But they're not taking into account the passion, the detail orientation, the staffing requirements—which are tremendous. It isn't as glamorous as it might seem. It's very humbling."

Apparently so. Scherber's next move was to quit the New York culinary arts circuit and travel through France in search of good bread. She was on the road for two years, tasting, querying, experimenting, ruminating—essentially living and breathing bread.

It paid off. When she returned, Scherber knew how to craft a glorious loaf. She could coax simple dough into crusty, crisp baguettes. And she worked wonders with semolina, golden raisins and fennel; whole wheat and walnuts; and earthy black olives. She gathered $150,000 in capital from family, friends and associates, and opened the doors of a sparkling new bakery.

Then the hard work began. "It took about two years for the business to really catch on—for people to discover us, try the bread and know it was good," Scherber explains. Meanwhile, running the new venture wasn't easy. "The first year especially, I had to cover a lot of different shifts myself because I couldn't afford to hire a manager. Sometimes I was covering the night shift and the early shift, and I found that I was slowly becoming more and more depressed."

The antidote? Hanging in there. "Around my one-year anniversary, I hired someone to help me in the office," says Scherber. "She took over a lot of things for me, and that made a huge difference." Business picked up substantially around the two-year mark, when Amy's Bread began attracting positive press. "*The New York Times* reviewed us, then *New York* magazine named us one of the 10 best bakeries in New York. That legitimized us with all the chefs and restaurants, and the business took off."

So much so, in fact, that Scherber has become a celebrity of sorts. She wrote a cookbook, *Amy's Bread* (William Morrow) in 1996. She's also hosted a baking show on the TV Food Network. With two thriving retail locations, Scherber admits that expansion is probably inevitable for her company. And she hasn't lost touch with the basic joy that got her into the business.

"Scoring the bread, shaping baguettes, seeing the bread going into the oven, coming out, smelling it, hearing the crust cracking—I find it soothing," she says.

Adam Pisoni, 22
Matthew D'Andria, 23
David Pisoni, 25
David Simon, 35

Cyber Nation

WHAT THEY DO: Full-service Internet
    development
HOME BASE: Santa Monica, California
FOUNDED: 1995
START-UP COSTS: $200,000 to $250,000
1997 SALES: Over $1 million
1998 PROJECTIONS: $3 million

From Arizona, it looked like a sane enough idea. Move to L.A. Start an Internet development company. Make a zillion dollars. College students and childhood friends Matthew D'Andria and Adam Pisoni were less than enthralled with school. They looked across the vast desert separating Scottsdale from Los Angeles and saw the glint of opportunity.

So they moved. Only in retrospect are the obstacles clear. "We didn't have any of the advantages that other [new media] companies have here," says D'Andria. "We didn't have millions of dollars. We didn't have entertainment backgrounds. We didn't have a list of contacts to call for financing. It was tough."

Talk About A Webolution

"It's funny. When we were younger, you were [considered] a nerd if you were involved with computers. Today, though, you're not—you're actually cool."

—ADAM PISONI

But the partners were tougher. They landed plenty of small assignments to keep them going, then got the contract to produce a Web site for video game developer Capcom Entertainment. Since then, they've attracted numerous high-profile clients, including Honda Motor Co., Sony Pictures and Nissan. Along the way, they acquired two partners, Pisoni's brother David and the company's attorney-turned-co-owner David Simon.

Three years into the business, Cyber Nation's prospects have improved dramatically. But the Internet industry remains a fast-paced and competitive one. Cyber Nation's main strength lies in its ability to stay ahead of the cutting edge, says Adam Pisoni.

"Every time a new technology comes out, we're expected to know it because the client is going to ask about it," Adam says. "So it's a constant learning process."

Not that they limit themselves to a learning curve. "In addition to keeping up with the industry, we're trying to be innovators ourselves," says D'Andria. Among the company's brainstorms: CyberStore, an online commerce application for selling goods and services over the Web.

Here, youth seems to be a major advantage. "Our team and our corporate culture is what enables us to go with the innovation in the industry—and allows us to innovate ourselves," says D'Andria. "Everyone here is really young. They're just out of college—top of their classes. We do everything by committee. And we have a lot of energy."

If Cyber Nation realizes even a fraction of its potential, it'll need energy. "What we're seeing today is only scratching the surface of how people can be connected around the world," says Adam. "The possibilities are unlimited—up to the day when everything from your refrigerator to your computer to your telephone answering machine is going to be connected to the Internet."

Jeff Haugen, 27
Tim Cady, 29

J.T. Tobacconists

WHAT THEY DO: Sell top-quality cigars wholesale and at two retail locations; maintain part ownership of cigar catalog *J.T. Cullen*

HOME BASE: Minnetonka, Minnesota

FOUNDED: 1995

START-UP COSTS: Over $10,000

1997 SALES: $2.2 million

1998 PROJECTIONS: $2.7 million

Photo© Mitchell & Witchell

As Jeff Haugen and Tim Cady peered into the window of a vacant store in Minnetonka, Minnesota, they saw more than just hardwood floors, a tin ceiling and antique detailing. They saw their future.

"It was only 450 square feet," says Haugen. "It was in the wrong part of town and it needed a lot of renovation. But we knew it would be the perfect place [to sell] retail cigars and accessories."

Staying Up In Smoke

"In retail, you're only as good as your next day's sales at the till. You never want to lose what you've worked so hard to build—and I think that's what keeps us going."

—JEFF HAUGEN

Not only was it the right place, but the partners were there at the right time—just as interest in quality cigars was being sparked nationwide. It was an exhilarating—but volatile—time. On the one hand, consumer demand was heating up. On the other hand, supply lines were about to go up in smoke.

"[Cigar] manufacturers had so much demand, they had trouble keeping up," says Cady. When established accounts began complaining that new operators were eating into the dwindling supply, many manufacturers stopped accepting new business. "We established our relationships with suppliers just in time," says Cady.

Just in time, that is, to realize the vision they had when they peered into that storefront window. The partners' retail concept goes beyond shelves and counters. It includes deluxe smoking lounges, cigar vaults for rent, and walk-in humidors. The idea is not simply to sell cigars, but to cultivate a love for the experience of smoking.

So far, the idea has been successful, but entrepreneurship has not been without its challenges. "It's been a daily struggle with cash flow," says Cady. And during the harsh Minnesota winters, luring people in for a casual smoke has been no mean feat.

Yet it's precisely those challenges that have made J.T. Tobacconists a commercial success. The company's wholesale division came about in response to slow winter sales. "We started hitting liquor stores, bars and restaurants [to sell cigars] because we needed some additional outlets to sell product during the months we couldn't rely on people to come in and buy," says Cady. "When sales get low, you've got to find new ways to sell; you've got to be willing to go out there and hit the streets. It takes strength and the will to survive. We can really kick ourselves in the butt when we have to."

Then again, they can also appreciate a fine cigar when the occasion calls for it—and that's often enough. "We're constantly doing taste tests," says Haugen. "We're searching for new products all the time. It's very important [that we] know the product inside and out, and that's why we've tried everything that's been placed on our shelves."

Not that sampling the inventory is such a drag. "We still sit down at the end of the day and enjoy a fine cigar," says Cady. "Just as we always have."

Photo© Randall Ball

Andrew Segal, 32

Boxer Property

WHAT THEY DO: Own and manage more than 50 office buildings in greater Dallas and Houston

HOME BASE: Houston

FOUNDED: 1992

START-UP COSTS: $1.2 million

1997 SALES: $25.5 million

1998 PROJECTIONS: $37.5 million

When Andrew Segal blew into town, Dallas was a ghost of its former self. The oil boom had gone bust, and the commercial real estate market had been all but dead for 10 years. But Segal didn't see the depression. He saw big, beautiful buildings priced at 5 to 15 percent of their replacement cost. He saw potential. He saw his future.

"People thought I was crazy. But when you came from out of town and looked at these structures, you had to believe they were worth more than the prices they were asking for them," Segal explains. "There were unprecedented deals to be made, and I knew that if the purchase was strong enough, it would cover a lot of the learning curve."

So Segal took a leap of faith—hand in hand with his recently divorced mother, who signed over every dollar she had to help back her son's new venture. Because of the condition of Texas' economy and the savings and loan crisis of the '80s, finding traditional bank financing was pretty much impossible. "Any bank that had any taste for real estate by definition had gone belly up," says Segal. "I did what I used to call dialing for dollars. I called everyone I knew and asked them to invest." Hundreds of phone calls and $1.2 million later, Segal was in business.

You're The Foundation

" There's a responsibility you take home every night with you when you have your own company. People tend to look at the upside, but it's hard for most people to understand the fear that you face, even when your company is doing well. But the fear is a motivator, and I guess it's good. It keeps your feet on the ground."

Owning an entire building brought a sense of prestige, but it was fleeting. "I raised enough money to buy the building, but I didn't have any money to fix it up," Segal recalls. "It was like an apprenticeship; I had to do everything myself. I was working 14 to 15 hours a day, running around in shorts and a T-shirt because I couldn't afford air conditioning. I would call it a mom and pop, but there weren't even that many people."

In time, though, Segal managed to lease the space. Tenants made improvements. Cash flow began turning around. And Segal bought another building—and another, and another. Today, Boxer Property owns more than 50 buildings in and around Dallas and Houston, and acquires a new property approximately every three weeks.

Segal no longer tends to everything himself, of course. Some 200 employees keep the business humming. Still, the foundation upon which he started the company sticks with him.

"When you start out doing everything, you know how to do everything," he says. "That's an advantage, but it's also a potential trap. For example, I find it very difficult to walk by a lease negotiation, because I know I can negotiate [the best deal possible]. But if I go in, I contaminate the process. It's almost like a recreational activity for me, but that's not a productive use of my time, and it's a problem for my staff. So I've had to let go of a lot of things that I enjoyed doing—even when I know they won't be done as well as if I had done them—because I can't do it all."

But then, if you can build a $25.5 million company in six years, you're probably doing enough. "One of the best things to come out of this," says Segal, "is that we've managed to rebuild family security from the ashes of my parents' divorce. People must have thought my mother was insane for putting all her money into this business. She was living in New York City at a friend's house, riding on the subway [to devote all her funds to the venture]. But it's all worked out."

Chapter 3

Cut To
The Chase

"I don't know
the key to success,
but the key
to failure
is trying to
please everybody."

—BILL COSBY

Ryan Smith, 25
Mike Fridgen, 23

International Student Tours

WHAT THEY DO: Coordinate and sell graduation travel packages to high school students

HOME BASE: Seattle

FOUNDED: 1997

START-UP COSTS: $150,000 to $200,000

1997 SALES: $1.5 million

1998 PROJECTIONS: $2.5 million

Mike Fridgen and Ryan Smith may have been young, but they knew there were enough tour companies in the world already. Plenty, in fact. When it came to meeting the unique needs of high school students, though, the competition was sparse.

"We'd been working for different companies who did [tour packages for students], so we were aware that the market existed," says Fridgen. "But there were maybe 10 companies in the country who specialized in graduation packages. After basically running [operations] for a company like this one, Ryan and I figured we could do the same thing for ourselves."

On The Move

"We think our strength comes from our team atmosphere, being young and excited about the future. We have a lot of college students working here; our oldest employee is 25. And he's the accountant."

—MIKE FRIDGEN

Smith and Fridgen had been partners before—first as co-founders of a T-shirt company, then as managers for the tour company. "We met as fraternity brothers at the University of Washington," says Fridgen. "We got along really well. We liked working together. And we both had learned a lot about the [student tour] business in our former jobs."

Contrary to what its name might imply, International Student Tours doesn't promise the world. Its packages focus on Hawaii and Mexico, and its marketing efforts focus on graduating seniors in Washington, Idaho and Oregon. Each school's students travel together, making the trip palatable to both kids and their protective parents.

"In this market, being young is a big advantage," reports Fridgen. "The more you can relate, the better." But youth has also presented its share of challenges. "In Mexico, we would meet with hotel managers to set up contracts and weren't taken seriously," says Fridgen. "We ended up bringing in an older advisor to participate in the negotiations with us."

The partners credit the University of Washington's program in entrepreneurship with a large measure of their success. Their mentor, entrepreneurship professor Shannon Hauser, has provided a wealth of assistance—including a referral to a sympathetic banker. Entrepreneurs with similar tour operations in other parts of the country have been helpful as well.

"Help is out there," says Fridgen. "Go through the university, the Small Business Administration, any place you can find other businesspeople. People are willing to help—especially young people who are trying to make something of themselves."

Matt Walsh, 33
Pam Walsh, 35
Greg Johnston, 31

Our Secret

WHAT THEY DO: Manufacture aromatherapy candles and accessories

HOME BASE: Albuquerque, New Mexico

FOUNDED: 1987

START-UP COSTS: $5,000

1997 SALES: Over $5 million

1998 PROJECTIONS: Over $10 million

Photo© Gamma Liaison/Cary Herz

It started simply enough. After a brief stint representing the products of various artists and craftspeople, Our Secret starting manufacturing its own line of distinctive candles. There were 25 products in all.

That was in 1987. Ten years later, Our Secret's line had mushroomed into 1,500 items. Sales had mushroomed proportionally but, as co-founder Greg Johnston points out, "We were becoming less and less profitable. The operational complexity of supporting that kind of line—the manufacturing requirements, the staffing, the collection of money—was causing our break-even [point] to sky-rocket."

They haven't exactly gone back to the drawing board. Johnston, his sister Pam Walsh, and Pam's husband, Matt, started the business as college students, living in the same house, working 16-hour days out of their garage, and making $25 a week. A return to that kind of minimalism would surely be too much.

Bright Idea

"If you have a good, simple idea, make it work. Then, when it does work, don't overcomplicate it."

—GREG JOHNSTON

But scaling back was clearly in order. And rebirth has been a major theme at Our Secret. In 1990, two days before a major trade show, a fire destroyed the company warehouse. It took 48 hours of continuous labor to rebuild inventory in time for the show. Five years later, another fire ravaged the company's new 43,000-square-foot facility. "We rebuilt our inventory in 10 days and had the largest shipping month in the history of the company," Johnston says.

Call it trial by fire—and call the verdict "successful." Though none of the partners wants to endure another raging inferno, Johnston does point out that each crisis has brought new perspective. "Any time there's an occurrence that could be perceived as negative, we look at it as an opportunity," he says. "Each time we've [had a fire], we've had to focus, to look at our need for core values and come together as a company."

Which is precisely what's happening now—minus the fire damage, of course. Johnston and the Walshes have pruned their line to 700 items and hope to streamline it even further. "We want to be an internationally recognized brand name," says Johnston. "To get there, we're going to have to stay focused on the dollars and sense of the business. We've learned that it's easy to add things, but very difficult to cut back."

John Pasmore, 36
Eddison Bramble, 35

New Image Media

WHAT THEY DO: Publish five beauty and
   trade magazines geared toward
   African-American women
HOME BASE: Hempstead, New York
FOUNDED: 1994
START-UP COSTS: $20,000
1997 SALES: $1.4 million
1998 PROJECTIONS: $2 million

Eddison Bramble and John Pasmore noticed something that some of New York's highest-paid editors missed. "African-American women were making more money and had become more assertive about their looks," says Bramble. But where were the beauty magazines that addressed their interests and needs? "Major-market [beauty magazines] had some coverage for African-American women, but it wasn't enough."

They knew they could do better. So Pasmore, whose background was in magazine publishing, and Bramble, a photographer, teamed up to launch their own publishing empire.

Hair-Raising

"I've done the research; I've read the stories. You see successful businessmen in [midlife] and they're doing well. But they don't talk about what they went through in their 20s and 30s to get there. The stories behind many of those men are long struggles before they finally hit it big."

—EDDISON BRAMBLE

"The original idea was to photograph hair styles for African-American women, so they could take the pictures to their hair stylists and [explain what they wanted done]," says Bramble. It was simple enough—but also explosive enough to provide the impetus for five magazines designed to meet the needs of African-American women: trade publications *Modern Hair, Elite Hair* and *Modern Short Cuts*, and beauty mags *Silhouette* and *Natural Style*.

Pasmore and Bramble know they're on the right track. Each magazine boasts a circulation of more than 50,000, and there's a strong European following. "Editorially, the magazines are catching on," says Bramble. "And media planners are receptive to what we're doing."

At the same time, "It was difficult getting started, and it's still difficult," Bramble reports. "Keeping the cash flow steady, getting funding, getting advertisers to understand the value of what we have to offer—it's a challenge every day. You see major titles spending $20 million to $30 million [on new magazine launches], and they still don't always succeed."

But major publishing companies don't have Pasmore and Bramble working tirelessly with minimal resources and maximum faith. Like every entrepreneur who's spotted a neglected niche and gone after it, Bramble and Pasmore are discovering the hazards of trying to reach an underserved market. There is skepticism, and nagging doubts about the viability of the concept. There is exhaustion, and worry about running out of steam before the job is done.

And there's hope in looking back over all the distance you've traveled and realizing there is more to you than you knew existed. "We're continually looking at the roadblocks and finding ways to get beyond them," says Bramble. "In the future, we think investors will see that we can do miracles with very little money—that's something attractive." And not something you see illustrated in the average beauty magazine.

Steven Grossman, 40

Just Kids Furniture Inc.

WHAT THEY DO: Operate a retail show-
  room devoted entirely to kids'
  furniture
HOME BASE: Farmingdale, New York
FOUNDED: 1993
START-UP COSTS: $250,000
1997 SALES: Over $2 million
1998 PROJECTIONS: $2 million

Imagine a store that's part Disneyland, part FAO Schwarz. Throw in a vast selection of juvenile bedroom furniture, and you get an idea of what Just Kids Furniture is all about.

"We're the largest kids' furniture store on the East Coast," says founder Steven Grossman.

But not just the biggest—also the most fun. Picture stuffed monkeys hanging from the ceiling, with giant giraffes and bears lurking nearby. Picture dozens of bedroom sets for kids on display. Imagine a world where kids not only come first, but where they rule.

At The Shop Till You Drop

" I'm supposed to be here six days a week, but I come in on my days off, too. It's fun. Coming home is work; work is fun."

This is what lured Grossman back into furniture retailing after his parents retired and closed the family furniture business. Grossman knew he wanted to apply his 15 years of industry experience to a new venture, but couldn't get excited about opening another generic furniture store. Then inspiration struck.

"I realized there was a void in the marketplace for juvenile furniture," Grossman explains. "[Other furniture stores] don't put kids in the spotlight. They don't put them center stage."

Grossman's hunch was confirmed when he approached furniture manufacturers with his business idea. "Some factories were reluctant to sell to me because they didn't understand the concept," he says. "Because there wasn't a store like this in the marketplace, they really weren't comfortable." Of course, "a lot of the companies that turned their backs on me in the beginning are knocking on my door now."

But Grossman has no time for I-told-you-so's. He's busy expanding. Though additional locations are still in the offing (but definitely planned), new product lines are already in the works, including custom window treatments and comforters and an increased emphasis on custom furniture.

"Every day is a different adventure," says Grossman. "That's the fun. That's the excitement."

Chris Lane-Kiersch, 36
Kimberly Lane-Kiersch, 36

Image Soup Inc.

WHAT THEY DO: Provide technology services, such as video production, computer networking, new media publishing, Web servers and more

HOME BASE: St. Louis

FOUNDED: 1991

START-UP COSTS: $2,000

1997 SALES: Over $2 million

1998 PROJECTIONS: $4 million

Photo Courtesy: Image Soup Inc.

Image Soup Inc.

Chris Lane-Kiersch was trying to get another business going when he came up with the idea for Image Soup. Lane-Kiersch had co-founded a computer hardware business aimed at the multimedia market. Trouble was, no one knew what multimedia was or how it might be used. To bolster sales, he decided to create multimedia presentations that would illustrate the technology's power. In the process, he uncovered a talent—and a demand—for production services that went beyond his former calling.

In short order, hardware seller Lane-Kiersch began his career as a multimedia mogul. Shortly after the company was formed, Chris' wife, Kimberly, joined the firm as a partner. In 1996, a national survey named Image Soup the fastest-growing tech firm in St. Louis; it had boasted 4,080 percent growth between 1991 and 1995.

Married, With Business

"Before we started this business, I didn't think it was very cool to work with your spouse. But working with Kim has been the best thing to come out of this experience. Any time someone starts a business, their spouse is doing something to allow that person to free up enough time to succeed. This way, we're on the ride together. And it's been kind of neat that I've been able to get on this ride with my best friend."

—CHRIS LANE-KIERSCH

What's the secret? Introducing cutting-edge technology to the often technology-starved Midwest. "Our idea has been to bring technology here at the same time it hits the West Coast," explains Chris. "This way, more production stays in the area and helps the local economy." Also, Fortune 500 companies based in the St. Louis environs get access to the same tools as their East and West Coast counterparts.

Maintaining a cutting-edge company takes some legwork, of course. One challenge is deciding which new technologies and applications to champion—a process that involves some trial and error. A boom in online commerce recently convinced the Lane-Kiersches to get into the business of developing online catalogs. Though that venue has been far from a flop, it also hasn't performed up to expectations.

"I visited seven companies in Seattle and Portland to see what they were selling and what their sales pitch was," says Chris. "What I saw was that they weren't doing the sales people thought they would. It cost me $10,000 to take the time off to make the trip, but it probably saved me $50,000 in lost effort. Now, we've decided to focus again on our core market—video editing—and we're projecting [1998] sales of $4 million," a nearly 100 percent increase over the previous year.

There are nontechnological reasons for Image Soup's success as well. Chief among them is the Lane-Kiersch team. When the couple married, they vowed to start a business together within five years. As luck would have it, says Kimberly, "We couldn't wait that long." Just a year later, opportunity knocked. The fact that Kimberly's background suited the new business well (she had worked in sales for a service bureau that sold images on slides) made the prospect of partnership especially appealing.

"We were both young," says Chris. "We had different skill sets. And we're both strong-headed. But with hard work, luck and a lot of perseverance, we've found a way to work together effectively."

John Puckett, 34
Kim Puckett, 34

Caribou Coffee

WHAT THEY DO: Run 115 coffeehouses,.
each with its own brand of local
flavor

HOME BASE: Minneapolis

FOUNDED: 1992

START-UP COSTS: $250,000

1997 SALES: $40 million

1998 PROJECTIONS: $60 million

The Caribou Coffee story begins atop Sable Mountain in Alaska. Kim and John Puckett made the long climb to the summit, drank in the view, and watched a herd of caribou thunder by. It was exactly the kind of experience that most people never find the time for, and exactly the kind of experience that inspires genius.

Caribou Coffee is many things. It's the place to go for a great cup of Joe. It's a gathering place for friends, a retreat for the harried, a local business that's making good. But it's also the direct product of that moment when John and Kim Puckett felt a true and simple connection to life's beauty.

Wake Up And Smell It

"I meet a lot of people who say, 'I'm really envious of you. I wish I could start my own business.' I don't know if they're waiting for someone or something to force them to do it, or if they aren't the kind of people who should start businesses. We spent a year working on this idea before we got started—and it's important to do the planning and the studying. But you have to realize there's no right time to jump in, and it's a mistake to wait too long."

—JOHN PUCKETT

And here's what Caribou Coffee isn't: An homage to Starbucks. In a world where it sometimes seems that every street corner and strip mall, every gas station and airport concession stand is occupied by a Starbucks or one of a zillion knockoffs, Caribou Coffee stands true.

And therein lies its strength. "Starbucks has been a competitor since the first day we started the business, and they're a good competitor," says John. "But we have a different approach. We're like Ben & Jerry's to their Häagen-Dazs. We've always had a real neighborhood emphasis, and people like that feeling. We've always been—and still are—a local company."

Pouring on the local flavor wasn't difficult when the Pucketts had a single store in Edina, Minnesota, which they launched in 1992. They had met as students at the Amos Tuck School of Business at Dartmouth College, had announced their engagement on graduation day, and had built impressive careers as up-and-comers in corporate America. Entrepreneurship was their answer to what John describes as a life in which "we were both earning a lot of money but were really miserable."

Starting Caribou changed all that, but it didn't necessarily herald the beginning of a stress-free existence. Three months after they opened their doors, the Pucketts picked up the newspaper and read that Starbucks was coming to the Twin Cities. It was time to get serious or get out of the coffee business.

John went about the task of raising the money they'd need to expand like crazy; Kim held down the fort by handling operations. That marked the kickoff to six years of raising capital, expanding the territory, refining the concept, nurturing the culture, and looking the giant right in the eye—all with the kind of focus only vision can provide.

Says John, "As the business grows, you go through stages. At first, it's hard physically. You're like a triathlete; you're doing everything yourself. Then you bring in experts and you delegate, and you end up getting away from some of the things that brought you joy in the first place. What we've found is that it's important to stay in touch with that joy."

Chapter 4

Break The Rules

"All great truths
are blasphemies."

—GEORGE BERNARD SHAW

Greg Maples, 35

High Tech Burrito Corp.

WHAT THEY DO: Serve up burritos with a conscience—fresh ingredients, bold flavors, minimal indigestion; 115 locations

HOME BASE: San Rafael, California

FOUNDED: 1986

START-UP COSTS: $80,000

1997 SALES: Over $10 million

1998 PROJECTIONS: $10 million

Greg Maples started out as a long shot. At 23, his primary work experience came from a stint in the U.S. Marine Corps. He was entering the wildly competitive world of food service, yet he had no particular restaurant background. In fact, most of what he knew about burritos came from having eaten them.

The whole idea of starting a business was irrational. And, truth be told, that was a big part of its early attraction. Unlike most young entrepreneurs, Maples didn't start out brimming with enthusiasm. He started out numb.

"After getting out of the Marines, my idea was to go to business school," Maples recalls. "But then my mother was murdered. I couldn't concentrate on school. I needed to be doing something concrete, something I could throw myself into."

Spice Of Life

"Since I didn't have a formal education, I had to think differently—but that wasn't a disadvantage. If I had listened to the naysayers, I never would have done this. You have to learn to listen to your own instincts."

So Maples spent $80,000 of his inheritance on launching a modest burrito stand—modest, that is, except in food quality. High Tech Burritos weren't the gut busters most people knew and consumed guiltily. They were made with fresh salsas, grilled meats, beans that actually tasted like beans. They were delicious. Irrationally delicious.

And so successful that Maples soon detected interest that went beyond the usual customer curiosity. "I had people showing up in limousines, wanting to take me to lunch," he says with a laugh. "I listened politely to what they had to say, but I never took any of them up on their offers [to buy the business, franchise or invest]. I could see that [to them] I was a young guy with only a little experience; I wouldn't have lasted long. And I had so many other ideas—I knew I hadn't completely exhausted my growth [as an entrepreneur]."

Good call. As it turned out, the inexperienced Maples had potential even he could not have predicted. Not only is his culinary vision received heartily in the San Francisco Bay area, but so is his talent as a leader.

"I've won an employer of the year award in Berkeley," says Maples. "That's really tough to do." The company's benefits include health care for all hourly employees, an employee stock ownership program, a policy of promoting from within, and general respect for employees as individuals. For example, says Maples, High Tech Burrito buys top-of-the-line equipment and uses all the best ingredients in its food. "That's important because it [results in] food that customers want to eat, but also because the people who work for you need to feel some pride in what they're doing," says Maples. "I can't babysit everybody who works here. But by giving them ownership of what they're doing, they care about the business, too.

"A lot of businesses say that the customer comes first," says Maples. "We think the employee is number one—and that if the employees are number one, they're going to treat the customers well."

With this kind of analytical thinking, Maples would have been a shoo-in for a business degree. But then, being the dark horse has its rewards, too.

Kirk Perron, 34

Jamba Juice Co.

WHAT THEY DO: Retail fruit smoothies with nutritional "juice boosts"
HOME BASE: San Francisco
FOUNDED: 1990
START-UP COSTS: $200,000
1997 SALES: $50 million
1998 PROJECTIONS: $60 million

Photo© Linda Sue Scott

71

It's not the lively purple and green graphics or the quaint sight of wheat grass growing in the display case that gets you first. It's the scent of oranges, so piquant and insistent that your mouth puckers and your stomach starts grumbling in sync with the blenders. You are in smoothie heaven. You are swirling in a vortex of delicious dilemmas. Do you want raspberry, strawberry, banana and orange? Passion fruit, mango, peach, strawberry and pineapple? Echinacea to charge up your immunity? Ginseng to boost your energy? Whichever way you go, you will leave Jamba Juice positively vibrating with health.

Liquid Assets

I I'm surprised there aren't more companies creating a culture beyond selling, a soulful experience for the customer. That's been the basis for our success."

Forget everything you learned in Marketing 101. In Kirk Perron's vision of 21st-century marketing, advertising isn't king. Though Jamba Juice Co. does have a marketing program, founder and CEO Perron knows that no direct mail, coupon-driven, broadcast-based, image-enhancing stunt will outperform the real hook at his outrageous fruit juice and smoothie stores. His secret: *It's the experience, stupid.*

"We didn't invent smoothies or fresh-squeezed juices," Perron says, "but we've created a niche by focusing on a sensory experience."

What's so ingenious about that? Nothing, unless you consider that Jamba Juice has grown from a single unit— originally called Juice Club—in the sleepy central California town of San Luis Obispo to 75 locations in only seven years—or unless you realize that Jamba faithfuls include Starbucks Coffee's Howard Schultz and Microsoft cofounder Paul Allen, both of whom have invested in the company.

In a universe that is wise to every kind of marketing ploy, Perron's experience-driven philosophy just might be the hardest sell going. Let everyone else promise the moon. Jamba Juice skips the promises and delivers—again and again.

Perron's cutting-edge perspective doesn't come from a marketing text, but from his own experience. The Jamba Juice story began in 1990, when a health-crazed Perron decided to turn his "juicing" habit into a business. At the time he hardly envisioned whipping the nation into a juice-guzzling frenzy, but Juice Club's high-quality, high-energy offerings became so popular that expansion was inevitable.

Juice Club tried its hand at franchising in 1993, but quickly changed its plan so that the company could maintain better control of the growing retail network. Instead, an infusion of capital from equity partners enabled Juice Club to shore up its strengths and gear up for new markets.

Though the Juice Club formula was successful, Perron felt it could use a little tweaking to compete in an increasingly crowded environment. So Juice Club got itself some *jamba*—the term comes from a West African word for "celebration"—and added a hipper, more global feeling. A sterile, health-food-store atmosphere has given way to vibrant purple, green, orange and hot pink, and natural wood.

Yet the core philosophy is the same. "This business may look like one where you can buy a few blenders and make a fortune, but it's more than that," Perron maintains. "The reason that our company exists is not simply to make money. We're providing enrichment to our customers' daily lives. People aren't stupid." Nor, he adds, are they susceptible to the same old marketing hype. "They know what's real."

Tracy Mikulec, 34
Jacob Knight, 30
Mike Freihofer, 32

World Oceans Media

WHAT THEY DO: Publish five magazines—*Wave Action Surf, Plow Snowboard, Pit Bodyboard, Launch Wakeboard* and *Wide Open Motocross*
HOME BASE: San Clemente, California
FOUNDED: 1993
START-UP COSTS: $10,000
1997 SALES: $2.9 million
1998 PROJECTIONS: $3.5 million

Somebody should have told Mike Freihofer, Jacob Knight and Tracy Mikulec that three surfers with no money, no office, and only a few years of business experience simply can't launch a successful magazine empire. That simple advice would have saved the trio from what Freihofer calls "the roller-coaster ride of starting a business."

Riding Tandem

"The hardest thing is transmitting your enthusiasm to other people. In a nonfinanced start-up, you have to know that everyone around you is willing to die for the project. If we have a secret to our success, it's our people. The good product and the money we make is the result of the hard work and care we put into what we do."

—MIKE FREIHOFER

But it would also have prevented them from becoming the publishers of five action-oriented magazines with a combined circulation of 320,000 and sales of nearly $3 million. "There's something to be said for ignorance, because if we'd known what was involved in starting a [publishing company], we would never have tried it," says Freihofer.

Not that the three friends were elated in their former careers. Freihofer had the good fortune to work for a surfing magazine, but he wasn't exactly raking in the bucks. "The magazine job wasn't paying the bills, so I was working part-time at a bike shop," he says. There he met Knight, who had a degree in finance and was, as Freihofer puts it, "also horrendously underemployed." The two began cooking up plans to start a surfing publication of their own. Freihofer called his former roommate Mikulec, a graphic designer, to see if he knew anything about putting a magazine together. Mikulec not only did but also agreed to join the motley crew.

Though they estimate start-up costs at $10,000, in reality the three partners didn't have much investment money. They raised the capital they needed by persuading advertisers to pay in advance.

They also kept expenses low by operating out of Freihofer's house for the first two years. "That was brutal," he recalls. "I had photographers knocking on the doors at 6 in the morning, not realizing that it was our home."

The World Oceans Media story isn't a tale of glamour from beginning to end, but the company has taken on some of the trappings of success—dedicated office space, for example, and a real staff. And if Freihofer, Knight and Mikulec aren't the kind of suit-wearing stiffs that run traditional magazine empires, they are three entrepreneurs who now have a clue about what it takes to be media moguls.

Though Freihofer admits that starting out with more money and a bit more experience might have been helpful, he also observes that real entrepreneurial experience is the best possible education. "It seemed like there were a million times when it didn't look like we were going to make it," he says. "But you just persevere. You invest so much financially and emotionally that it's hard to give up. You just say, 'I'm so deep into this that I might as well keep going. I don't have anything more to lose.'"

Ruffin Slater, 40

Weaver Street Market

WHAT THEY DO: Run a cooperative
natural foods grocery
HOME BASE: Carrboro, North Carolina
FOUNDED: 1988
START-UP COSTS: $500,000
1997 SALES: $5.7 million
1998 PROJECTIONS: $6.8 million

Photo© Duane Salstrand

Ruffin Slater was like any entrepreneur with a hot idea. He was visiting banks, calling on private investors, racking his brain, pounding the pavement. Ahead were plenty of long hours, sleepless nights, challenges he would not have imagined possible. His story is just like any other entrepreneur's—except for one thing: Slater doesn't own his business.

Because of its founder's efforts, Weaver Street Market not only exists, but it flourishes in the college community of Carrboro. Also thanks to Slater, the market belongs to its employees and some 3,000 consumer members through a cooperative ownership arrangement.

Beet Of A Different Drum

"You really have to believe in the business, even when the feedback you're getting is that what you're trying to do can't be done. Eventually, you will find an alternative way to get there."

Nonownership has its advantages. For one thing, Slater says, "A lot of [investors] were interested in the alternative structure of the business. In this town, a lot of people [associated with the University of North Carolina] were disposed to this kind of concept. I couldn't have raised the money if I didn't have the cooperative structure."

There's also a marketing benefit, if you want to call it that. "We're trying to set up a different kind of relationship between the business and the community," explains Slater. "We're striving to break down the mistrust people sometimes have of the places where they shop." In fact, Weaver Street Market patrons go beyond mere trust; many take an active role in ensuring the market's success. "If one of our consumer owners sees someone shoplifting, they bring it to our attention immediately," says Slater. "It's their business, too."

Employees are similarly motivated. "The people who

work here are much more interested in the business because they are part-owners," Slater reports. "It's actually made it easier to manage the business."

On the downside, Slater isn't increasing his personal wealth at the level most entrepreneurs might expect. But he's pleased with the payoff he is getting. "The [dividend] for me is seeing how big a difference the store makes in the community," he says. "People really respond to the friendliness, and the way the store is responsive to their needs. My rewards come from [emotional sources], since the financial rewards in a cooperative business are not what they would be in a conventional business or partnership. But those rewards are valuable."

Ken Seiff, 34

Pivot Rules

WHAT THEY DO: Manufacture golf
clothes you can wear off the
course

HOME BASE: New York City

FOUNDED: 1991

START-UP COSTS: $5,000

1997 SALES: Over $10 million

1998 PROJECTIONS: Not available

Photo© Catherine Gibbons

People who start golfwear companies should know a thing or two about golf. Ken Seiff would agree, although he isn't one to hit the links. "I've played a couple of times, but when I started the company I was not a golfer," he says. "Technically, I'm still not a golfer."

Seiff does, however, make some of the best-looking golf clothing on the course. To do it, he didn't need a scratch game; he needed a smidgen of fashion sense—just a smidgen. In 1991, when Seiff (then a management consultant) launched the company, golfing attire consisted of putrid plaids, hideous hues, and fibers so artificial it was a wonder that grass didn't wither in its wake.

That was fine for the over-50 crowd. But as Seiff noticed more and more young adults picking up the game, he sensed dissatisfaction—nay, *disgust*—with traditional golf lines. The gap wasn't simply one of age; it was also one of attitude.

All In The Game

"We work hard here, but we have fun. We've put an electric massage chair into the reception area. We've made an office that looks like a living room—and why? Any time you've got a group of people who are having fun, they have much more creativity, much more longevity, and much more focus. Besides, I've never been a corporate guy. I much prefer not having to shave every day. I like wearing a polo shirt to work. This company is relaxed and casual, which is what we're selling to customers."

"These golfers play for fun," says Seiff. "They're more relaxed, casual, and younger. They don't expect to play golf like Greg Norman, and they aren't especially interested in dressing like Greg Norman. They aren't preoccupied with getting a 72. They're happy just getting a couple of great shots and being outside with their friends."

What's the difference? Casual golfers don't want an entire wardrobe of clothing that's only appropriate for the course. "When we went out and interviewed golfers to find out what they wanted, we learned that they were wearing the same clothes on the golf course and off," says Seiff. That meant clothing had to meet regular fashion standards. Casual golfers also weren't wedded to their pro shops like their more traditional counterparts. "Part of our strategy was looking at more convenient distribution channels, such as department stores and catalogs," says Seiff.

The strategy was a winner. Pivot hit $2.3 million in sales its first year—far more than Seiff had imagined in his most optimistic projections. A lucky shot? Not when you consider his commitment to his concept.

"When we hit the stores, I went around to every store and spent seven days a week talking to salespeople, talking to customers, explaining what our clothes were about, asking for feedback, and basically helping the retailers move the product," says Seiff. "After six weeks, we had sold our entire inventory and had to have more made. We had incredible sell-through.

"It's not unusual for a designer to visit a store—for a trunk sale, for example. But it is unusual for them to do it seven days a week for six weeks. The buyers in the stores really appreciated it. And customers appreciated it, too. It put a face behind the product."

And though it isn't the face of a famous golfer—or even of someone who golfs much—customers don't seem to mind. Seiff may not be able to improve your swing, but he's one of the few people out there who can make you look better trying.

Chapter 5

If This Were My Company . . .

"You must be the change you wish in this world."

—MAHATMA GHANDI

Dave Kapell, 36

Magnetic Poetry

WHAT THEY DO: Create and market make-your-own-poetry kits; line includes 50 kits and related products

HOME BASE: Minneapolis

FOUNDED: 1993

START-UP COSTS: $100

1997 SALES: $6 million

1998 PROJECTIONS: $6.5 million

Photo© Doug Knutson

Magnetic Poetry

Dave Kapell had a song in his heart, and he couldn't put it into words. He struggled. He labored. He wrote down interesting words, cut them into individual pieces, and tried arranging and rearranging them into workable songs. Good idea, but then the allergy-plagued Kapell would sneeze, and his best work would go flying.

Kapell was not defeated. He pasted the words onto magnets and stuck them to a pizza tin, and eventually to the refrigerator door. Then he noticed that visiting friends couldn't keep their hands off his words. They'd stand at the refrigerator, creating poems of their own.

Perhaps Kapell was onto something. He bought $100 worth of supplies, made up 100 sets of magnetic words, and took them to a local crafts fair. They sold out in three hours.

Say It Again

"English is a great major because it generally makes you a smarter person. That's everything."

That was how Dave Kapell—"administrative guy" for a produce wholesaler and amateur songwriter—began the process of teaching America how to express itself. "A need in myself turned out to be a need for a lot of people," says Kapell. "Americans have a deep-seated need for expression—for good, strong, potent language. We all do."

Magnetic Poetry contains a genius that exceeds the sum of its parts. On the surface, it's just a box of little magnetic words. But combining them into a satisfying thought is remarkably easy, so that even the hopelessly inarticulate can create memorable images and witty phrases. "They're like training wheels," Kapell explains. "They provide the help a lot of people need."

Apparently so. To date, Magnetic Poetry has sold over a million kits, including kids' versions, theme versions and foreign language versions. There's even "Poetry Paint," latex paint that contains enough iron powder to make painted surfaces as magnet-friendly as your refrigerator.

"[Launching Magnetic Poetry] was like giving birth to a prodigy," Kapell says. "It was simultaneously easy and difficult. On the one hand, the product sold itself—and continues to sell itself. On the other hand, keeping up with it and nourishing it has been a challenge." There is competition in the form of cheap knockoffs. There's the ongoing job of keeping retailers—and their customers—interested. And there are growing pains: the cost of technology, expanding operations, the rigors of building a solid brand name.

There's a payoff as well. Kapell is pleased to have installed "Poetry Walls"—20-by-8-foot magnetic walls loaded with Magnetic Poetry—in public spots around the country. Consider them his contribution to public literacy.

And he's touched by the letters he receives from Magnetic Poetry users. One wrote that her 17-year-old autistic son is forming sentences for the first time with the help of Magnetic Poetry. "Psychologists have written about having breakthroughs with abuse victims with the use of this product," says Kapell. "We're actually doing something that contributes to people's lives. Obviously, that's rewarding."

Steve Rosenstein, 38
Andi Rosenstein, 37

Fitigues Inc.

WHAT THEY DO: Manufacture and
market casual clothing that com-
bines pajama comfort with style;
run 26 retail outlets, a catalog
and a Web site

HOME BASE: Chicago

FOUNDED: 1988

START-UP COSTS: $20,000

1997 SALES: $21 million

1998 PROJECTIONS: $30 million

Photo© Grant H. Kessler

Steve and Andi Rosenstein grew up in the surfwear industry—in more ways than one. For years, the husband and wife worked as sales reps for a surfwear company, where the outdoor lifestyle—surfing, playing volleyball and hanging out at the beach—made its wake in the world of fashion. But as the Rosensteins (and the rest of the baby boom generation) matured, new forces came into play.

"As [the baby boomers] began to grow up and get real jobs, our interests began to change," says Steve. "We [had families] and began spending more and more time at home with the kids."

No Sweat

"Being naïve when you're young can work in your favor. There were a lot of times that we were so naïve, we just kept going—even when, now, I might see the same situation and say, 'We're in trouble.' Then, we were too persistent, too passionate to see it."

—STEVE ROSENSTEIN

Hanging out at home might not seem to present much of a fashion challenge, but couch potatoes everywhere know the dilemma: You want something supremely comfortable, but you don't want to be embarrassed if you have to answer the door or step out for a quick meal. "We saw a need for clothing that people could throw on and be comfortable wearing, but that still had some style," says Steve.

Andi made a few sketches to illustrate the point—sketches that, in feeling, probably aren't much different from the Fitigues of today. Here was high-quality cotton knitwear in loose, simple, fashionable shapes. The look was finished, not frumpy, but the feeling was pure pajamas—just the ticket for a nation of stressed-out, sleep-deprived, family-centered baby boomers.

Taking those sketches from the drawing board and into department stores wasn't a job for amateurs. Andi and Steve used their industry contacts to land accounts with Nordstrom, Marshall Field's and Bloomingdale's. Then they approached manufacturers, who agreed to accept payment directly from the retailers. That allowed the Rosensteins to finance their start-up without loans.

Launching a business on meager funds, meeting the demands of rapid growth, transforming the organization from a mom-and-pop into a midsized corporation, and keeping pace with changing lifestyles hasn't been easy for the Rosensteins, who also managed to start a family in their so-called spare time. But, Steve says, "Stepping up to the plate and making the company a success has been extremely rewarding."

So has making a statement about society's values, as Fitigues does in its own indirect way. "We're not trying to tell people that clothes are the most important thing in their lives," says Steve. "Other catalogs have pictures of beautiful models looking out over the cliffs at St. Tropez. That's not me, and it's probably not you. One of the things that's made us successful is that people who deal with us know they're dealing with real people."

Kevin Achatz, 44
Larry Gutkin, 39
Larry Wojciak, 40

Ingear Corp.

WHAT THEY DO: Manufacture backpacks, sports bags and water-sports accessories

HOME BASE: Lincolnshire, Illinois

FOUNDED: 1994

START-UP COSTS: $850,000

1997 SALES: $39.5 million

1998 PROJECTIONS: $52 million

Photo© Andy Goodwin

They were three smart guys with the collective talent to earn millions. The problem: They were earning millions for someone else. So when philosophical differences with their former employer proved irreconcilable, executives Kevin Achatz, Larry Gutkin and Larry Wojciak resolved to create their own, similar company—only this time, they'd be in charge.

Call it a coup for disgruntled employees everywhere. Just four years after the trio founded Ingear Corp., their backpacks, luggage, sports bags and accessories are on the shelves of Kmart, Wal-Mart, Target, Sears and Sports Authority stores nationwide.

The partners' experience clearly won the day. Without it, they probably wouldn't have been able to secure $850,000 in start-up funds from investors. And they prob-

High On The Tote

"Walking through airports and seeing people using our products; going to my son's school and seeing his classmates carrying our products around—that's really great. We got into this because we wanted to make a difference, and [when you see your product out there], you see that you are."

—LARRY WOJCIAK

ably wouldn't have been able to land mass merchandising giant Kmart as their first big account. "Looking back, I would say it was impossible [for a start-up to win the Kmart account]," says Wojciak. "But we went in there with an exciting new product at a great price. And, of course, we already had good relationships with people, which was a tremendous help."

At bottom, the reasons for Ingear's success are simple. "We've got an exceptional product with the highest possible quality and impeccable delivery," says Wojciak. It's a formula that's easy to articulate, but tough for all but the swiftest newcomers to deliver.

Societal trends have also played a key role in Ingear's success. "We've become a more mobile society, and with that mobility comes the need to carry stuff around with you," Gutkin says. Keeping pace with the market isn't simply a matter of cranking out the basics, though. Gutkin attributes Ingear's strength to its ability to respond to a variety of interests within the market. For example, Ingear's line includes carrying cases for in-line skates, and bags for sports enthusiasts to tote their water bottles.

Although forming a partnership with co-workers has potential risks, the combination of Achatz's finance and marketing wizardry, Gutkin's international experience, and Wojciak's sales and marketing talent—in tandem with the partners' natural rapport—has been nothing but productive. And according to Gutkin, it beats being employed.

"[Starting a business is] certainly a roller-coaster ride," says Gutkin. "There are days when you're down, and there are days when you're higher than a kite." Still, he says he wouldn't go back unless someone held a gun to his head. "Even then," he adds, "I'd have to ask what caliber the bullet was."

Andrew Tuchler, 30

Ultimate Parking

> WHAT THEY DO: Provide valet parking service for more than 50 businesses in Greater Boston
>
> HOME BASE: Boston
> FOUNDED: 1989
> START-UP COSTS: $3,000
> 1997 SALES: Over $3 million
> 1998 PROJECTIONS: Over $4 million

Photo© Tracy Powell

Andrew Tuchler is a restless guy. In high school, he didn't settle for strictly academics. He got a job as a parking valet, then continued working part time while attending Northeastern University in Boston. But when the parking company didn't deliver on a promised promotion, Tuchler wouldn't settle for being a worker bee. He promoted himself—to founder of his own company.

Entrepreneurship proved to be a good use of Tuchler's energy. "I needed energy to build the business," he says. "And, being so young, I was able to do 16 hours a day, six days a week without crashing."

Driving Force

"I'm proudest of the reputation we've established in this community as successful, hardworking people."

Breaking into Boston's competitive valet parking business took persistence. Tuchler's turning point came when restaurateur Lydia Shire chose Ultimate Parking to provide valet services at her upscale eatery, Biba. "We had just started out, we only had one client, and we were competing [for Biba's business] with three or four larger valet companies," says Tuchler. "She saw something in us—the new kid on the block—and gave us the chance that made us what we are today."

Being an entrepreneur brought Tuchler's college career to a halt. "That was a disadvantage," he admits. "When problems have occurred, I haven't had the education [that might have told me how to handle them]. At the same time, nine years later I think the best education is the business itself—stumbling upon every possible business scenario and working through it. There are still always new things that come across my desk. That's what makes it challenging—and interesting."

Besides, a guy with Tuchler's kinetic tendencies doesn't

thrive in a rarefied, sedentary environment like school. He likes settling into the driver's seat and putting the wheels in motion—whether the vehicle is a client's Porsche or his own company.

Rhonda Lashen, 36

Fortunately Yours Inc.

WHAT THEY DO: Make and market customized fortune cookies
HOME BASE: Gahanna, Ohio
FOUNDED: 1992
START-UP COSTS: $1,000
1997 SALES: $1.2 million
1998 PROJECTIONS: Over $2 million

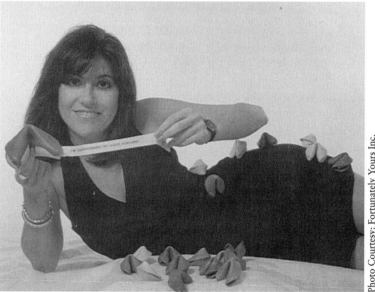

Photo Courtesy: Fortunately Yours Inc.

They were the perfect gift—small, intimate, unique. Rhonda Lashen was sold on giant fortune cookies. "I had ordered one as a gift, but when I called back to order a second time, the company had gone out of business," says Lashen, whose disappointment inspired her to think further—and, ultimately, to act.

"I thought [giant fortune cookies] were such a great gift idea that I decided to start making them myself," says Lashen. "I hired a [contract] baker and a printer, and started marketing."

Lashen's instincts were right—and wrong. There was indeed a market for giant fortune cookies, but Lashen found her true fortune when she branched out into new areas. First she discovered a niche market in personalized fortune cookies for bar and bat mitzvahs. From there, she moved into the corporate market. Fortune cookies bearing customized messages make a tasty marketing tool for banks, realtors, hotels and businesses of almost every kind.

Smart Cookie

"I've finally come to the point where I can accept the fact that I can't do everything. I used to be upset when I wasn't able to [take advantage of demand]. We'd have a great Valentine's Day, but I'd feel like I should have sold even more. Now I know you can only do so much."

"It's so hard for businesses to find that perfect marketing [vehicle] nowadays," explains Lashen. "If you can put a smile on someone's face, that's important."

Lashen's success doesn't stop with corporate clients. She does a brisk wedding trade, gets a flood of business around Valentine's Day, and is always open to unconventional uses of her product. Fortunately Yours' giant cookies are, Lashen points out, big enough to hold resumes or car keys. There is a limit, of course. "I had someone who wanted to put boxer shorts [in a giant cookie]," she says, laughing. "They wouldn't fit."

Which is not to say that Lashen is sorry she made the effort. "You always have to try new things," she says. "Some work, some don't, and you make mistakes. But you learn from your mistakes and move on."

And, if you're Lashen, you don't let anything get in the way of your enthusiasm. Six years into the business, Lashen is a little older and a little wiser, but no less effusive about her cookies. "You have to believe in your product," she says. "You can't sell something if you don't."

But then, what's not to believe? Lashen has taken cookies you can get at any Chinese restaurant in the country and made them valuable gifts, favors and promotional tools. By adding multiple flavors to her line, she's even made them more delicious. With savvy like this, you can see where her company is heading—even without reading the fortune.

Annette Quintana, 37
Victoria Quintana, 38
Excel Professional Services

WHAT THEY DO: Computer consulting
HOME BASE: Greenwood Village,
   Colorado
FOUNDED: 1990
START-UP COSTS: $55,000
1997 SALES: $20 million
1998 PROJECTIONS: $25 million

Photo© Patricia Bary Levy

Annette Quintana had already helped launch a computer consulting company when she began contemplating a launch of her own. She'd seen the long hours, the struggles, the stress. She'd been through it, only without the benefits of ownership. It wasn't easy to commit to starting her own business—knowing all the effort that would go into it—but the promise of ownership made the idea appealing. She would do it again, and this time the success would be hers.

Or, as it turned out, *theirs*—Annette was joined by her sister Victoria shortly after she founded Excel Professional Services in 1990. Since then, success has been relative. Not only have the sisters formed an effective partnership, but their father, a former high school teacher and real estate developer, is an investor in the company.

How It Computes

"We want to provide the highest level of service to our clients. We expect a high level of ethics and integrity. And we have a heart for our employees. All those little nuggets form the philosophy that's made us a success."

—Victoria Quintana

With Annette's direct experience and Victoria's background as a product manager for MCI, the sisters figured they had a good shot at making their company work. No one imagined, however, that Excel would be projecting $25 million in sales just eight years after its inception.

Least of all banks, who were initially reluctant to lend money to the Quintanas. "A lot of banks wanted our husbands to sign documents," says Victoria. "We really had to shop around to find banks that were willing to work with us on our own terms."

Working on their own terms has been a major theme for

the sisters, who credit their strong relationship with a large measure of the company's success. "We complement each other well," says Annette. "I tend to be more visionary, setting goals—more analytical. Victoria's more organized and has better people skills. That's a good combination."

Better still, it's a match that works away from the office as well. "We were both concerned going into this about the impact the business would have on our personal relationship—and the personal relationship was the priority," says Victoria. "But it's worked out really well. We're building homes four lots away from each other so our kids can grow up together."

Naturally, running a business with 230 employees and such major clients as US West, AT&T and Time Warner isn't without its struggles and stress. But this time, it comes with ownership and the opportunity to work with family. Annette Quintana is still taking care of business; she's just taking care of herself in the process.

Judy McDonald, 37
Irit Hillel, 36
Rosie Welch, 45

Jiro Inc.

WHAT THEY DO: Publish multimedia software for the crafts market

HOME BASES: Portland, Oregon, and Paris

FOUNDED: 1995

START-UP COSTS: $90,000

1997 SALES: Nearly $10 million

1998 PROJECTIONS: $30 million

Photo Courtesy: Jiro Inc.

Here was the problem: Hewlett Packard was selling a ton of color printers, but wasn't seeing the kind of usage it expected after the sale. Because sales of ink were most profitable, HP was looking for ways to encourage customers to use their printers.

Here was employee Judy McDonald's solution: Develop software that would enable people to use their computers and color printers to create customized craft projects, such as iron-designs for T-shirts. The right software would give users the push they needed to put the technology to work. McDonald pitched it to her boss at HP, and he declined.

"I was so disappointed," McDonald recalls. "My friend Irit [Hillel] was visiting for the day [from Paris] and we were driving around together. I asked her, 'Can you believe this? Here's this great product and it's not going to be produced.' And she said, 'We'll produce it.'"

Seeing It In Print

"As you move along in life, you buy into these ideas—*I need a house. I need a mortgage. I need a job.* But it's not necessarily true. You have a lot more freedom than you think."

—JUDY MCDONALD

McDonald was not convinced. She had a stable job, a promising career. "When you work for HP, you begin thinking that anything other than working for HP is too risky," says McDonald. Then came the phone call. "Irit had been to a trade show in Germany and saw that iron-on T-shirts were the big thing. 'We have to do this,' she said." This time, the idea stuck.

That was how McDonald and Hillel found themselves positioned outside computer stores on two continents, asking customers what they thought of the software idea. The response was so encouraging that even a cautious McDonald couldn't resist. She persuaded a friend, graphic designer

Rosie Welch, to join the team, and they began building PrintPaks. Their software runs the gamut, from kits that allow users to turn images into refrigerator art (using self-adhesive magnets) to packages for creating customized books, jewelry and party supplies.

"The scariest moment in the whole thing was quitting my job," says McDonald. "But about a week after I quit, I was sitting on my front lawn working on the business plan, and I said to myself, 'This is going to be OK. Even if I end up having to work at McDonald's, I can do that.'"

But burger-flipping wasn't in the picture. Finding a rep and getting the product into stores was a huge challenge. So was meeting financial demands. But PrintPaks had a life of their own. "Rosie's designs gave the software a real creative soul," says McDonald. Meanwhile, McDonald and Hillel worked tirelessly on marketing.

Their efforts paid off—not just in burgeoning sales but also by attracting the attention of Mattel, which recently acquired the company with the intention of keeping its current management team in control of the division (now named Jiro Inc.). The division will develop future products under the new label, Fashion Magic.

"[The aquisition] was an important move for us because it means that we're not bootstrapping it anymore," says McDonald. "We'll have more marketing money, and Mattel has fabulous distribution in kids' channels."

What the acquisition doesn't mean is that McDonald is back with the corporate program. In her three years of entrepreneurship, she's discovered something of a new self. "I told Mattel in negotiations that if they thought I would be there to climb the corporate ladder, they could forget it. [Entrepreneurship has] made me realize I like taking risks," she says. "I didn't see that in myself before.

"Now I realize that even if I had become president of HP, my impact would have been unclear. But when you have your own company, you really have a chance to do something different, something important. It shows you what you can really do with your life."

Chapter 6

I Did It My Way

"Some people
march to a
different drummer—
and some people
polka."

—UNKNOWN

Bob Baumann, 38

Around Your Neck Inc.

WHAT THEY DO: Men's image consulting and clothing sales
HOME BASE: Dallas
FOUNDED: 1991
START-UP COSTS: $8,000
1997 SALES: $1.7 million
1998 PROJECTIONS: $2.5 million

Photo© Robie Capps

Bob Baumann won't sell you the shirt off his back, but he'll sell you one just like it. Also for sale: his tie, shoes, belt and pants. Baumann draws the line at his boxers, though. That, he says, would just be embarrassing.

Welcome to the universe of professional image consulting and the domain of Bob Baumann, who was once so driven to get a great tie at a great price that he stumbled upon a business opportunity.

It began when Baumann, then a successful salesman, bought himself a $75 tie on his lunch hour. "Driving back to the office, I reached over and looked at that necktie and I thought, 'This is crazy. A piece of silk this size cost $75?' I knew it didn't cost that much to make," says Baumann. When he reached the office, he made a few phone calls and discovered that the same tie wholesaled for $18. "Eighteen dollars!" he cries. "Can you believe the markup on that?" He tried to buy a minimum order of five dozen on the spot, but without a resale number, he was foiled.

On The Rack

"I'm truly an entrepreneur, but I'm not a true businessman. I don't want to look at papers all day—sign this and sign that. I'm not good in meetings, either. Before you're four words into a question, I know what it's going to be and I'm on to the next thing. That's why I brought in a COO recently. I was forcing myself to do something I absolutely hate—running this company. Now, someone else can do that, and I can be the idea guy. That's what I'm good at."

No matter. Months later, when Baumann decided it was time to quit his sales job in favor of something more interesting, he remembered the markup on those ties and wondered if he could sell them. Not in a store, of course. Not conventionally. Here he was, a master salesman. How could he leverage that talent without incurring the cost of a retail location?

The answer was going directly to the customer. Baumann's first gig was a "tie show" in a conference room, where he sold 65 ties in a little more than an hour. "Back in the early '90s, neckwear sales were through the roof," says Baumann. "Times were tough and people could afford to buy three new ties when they couldn't afford three new suits."

As times changed—and Baumann's ambition grew—he added suits, jackets, shirts, pants and accessories. He discovered that men don't need a store to shop. In fact, they'd rather do without the store altogether. "There's never been a man who woke up on a Saturday morning and said, 'Hey, honey! Look! Brooks Brothers is having a sale! Let's go!'" Baumann says kiddingly. "Most people know, men hate to shop."

They also hate the mysteries of fashion, Baumann found. "Men do not like to be put into a situation where they don't know what's going on," he says of his clients, who trust him to point them in the right direction. "They don't know what [clothes] to buy, or what to put with what. When we tell them, they love it."

It's not just a question of knowledge; it's a matter of convenience. "There are more demands on people's time today than ever," says Baumann. "I don't walk out of the office until 7 o'clock. The last thing I want to do at that point is go to the mall to buy a shirt."

Baumann is betting that other men across the country couldn't agree more. He's franchising Around Your Neck and seeking to expand sales in the Dallas area by 30 percent in 1998—even as business attire becomes increasingly casual. "We're addressing that trend as well," says Baumann. "People are as confused about casual dressing vs. sloppy dressing as they've ever been [about clothes]." Until they meet Baumann, that is.

Barry Barr, 28

KAVU Inc.

WHAT THEY DO: Manufacture and market clothing for outdoor sports

HOME BASE: Seattle

FOUNDED: 1994

START-UP COSTS: $20,000

1997 SALES: $3 million

1998 PROJECTIONS: Over $4 million

KAVU stands for Klear Above, Visibility Unlimited. "It [describes] the perfect day," says Barry Barr, whose participation in several adventure sports led him to start the company that clothes fellow extreme athletes.

Not that Barr's experience with extreme temperatures is limited to his off hours. Before launching KAVU, Barr was a commercial fisherman in Alaska. "When you're on a fly bridge on the Bering Sea and the wind blows, your hat blows off. I got cold," Barr recounts dryly. "So I tried to come up with a hat that wouldn't blow off."

After spending some time, as he describes it, "just goofing around with the sewing machine," Barr invented the KAVU hat, which really did stay on, even in high wind—or high activity—situations.

All Work, More Play

"Even if you're working 7 to 6, you've got to get out and burn up that energy. Go out for a little while and do something—anything. I paraglide. I kayak. I mountain bike, ski, surf—you name it. I have lots of toys."

It was a hit. In the beginning, Barr sold the hats in "any place 10 people were." First on board were local specialty stores, then similar stores nationwide, and finally such major accounts as L.L. Bean and REI. Now, KAVU promotes its full line of cotton and canvas sportsgear to kayakers, rock climbers and mountain bikers worldwide.

"In Norway, we're bigger than Nike," jokes Barr.

Even at home, KAVU isn't doing so badly. Barr credits much of the company's success to its high standards. "We've been able to keep awesome quality because we manufacture domestically," he says. "We've been able to turn things around quickly that way, too. If there's a problem, we just pop down the street and fix it."

It doesn't hurt, either, that KAVU's staff is as young—

and wild—as its founder. "The average age here is 25," Barr reports. "Everyone's friends, and we all go out after work. But it's also competitive. We try to work hard and play harder."

Though fishing in Alaska might not appear to be direct training for entrepreneurship, Barr insists it was the best orientation around. "When you're out there on the Bering Sea and your engine cuts out, you better have three solutions to every problem," he says, "because the first two might not work."

Despite the inevitable challenges, growing KAVU has been tamer by comparison—and perhaps more rewarding. "When you're an entrepreneur, you get to work as long as you can without overtime pay," quips Barr. "But you also get the freedom to make decisions that count." Hats off to that.

Michael Baker, 32

Houndstooth Clothing Co. Inc.

WHAT THEY DO: Design and manufacture T-shirts and casual clothing that combine American nostalgia with old-fashioned standards of quality; two retail locations and wholesale accounts

HOME BASE: Fayetteville, Arkansas

FOUNDED: 1992

START-UP COSTS: $12,000

1997 SALES: Over $1 million

1998 PROJECTIONS: Not available

Photo Courtesy: Houndstooth Clothing Co. Inc.

When architect Michael Baker began designing T-shirts, he had confidence that the public would like them. It was the retailers he doubted. "I was very insecure that anyone else would want to sell my product," says Baker. "I couldn't imagine anyone saying to me, 'Sure, I'll sell your things in my store.'"

Happily, what Baker lacked in chutzpah he made up in diligence. Rather than pursuing retail accounts fruitlessly, he decided to open his own store—no chance of rejection there. Local college students took to the T-shirts in a major way, making Baker's Houndstooth Clothing Co. an instant hit. And after taking the shirts home, wearing them for a year, and finding they lasted like iron, enthusiasts returned again and again.

Clothes The Deal

"What gets your motor running is pulling people in the door and getting them to turn over part of their hard-earned paycheck. When that happens, you're walking on air."

Now sold online and by mail order, the Houndstooth line has expanded to include a variety of casual clothes for men and women—rugged T-shirts, sweatshirts, shorts and caps, bearing the Houndstooth logo, in stylish, classic colors. Baker's store, decorated with rich oak cabinets and wooden floors as well as antique sporting goods equipment, transports you to a magical yesteryear when personal service was the norm.

On the other hand, a computer station where shoppers can take time out to surf the Internet (and visit Houndstooth's Web site) lets you know that this company is firmly anchored in the future. And speaking of the future, Baker also plans to market the Houndstooth brand to select department stores.

If that sounds like a 180-degree turnaround, so be it.

Baker now believes the retailing expertise he and his company have developed will serve wholesale clients well. "We know an awful lot about marketing, merchandising and presentation [that we didn't know when we started]," says Baker. "Now, we can say to retailers, 'Here's our product and here's how we'd like you to sell it.'"

Baker's story is proof positive that nagging insecurities shouldn't stop you from pursuing an entrepreneurial dream. Building a million-dollar business from the ground up wasn't easy. "When I started this company, I just had pictures in my head of clothing I thought would sell," says Baker. "I couldn't read a balance sheet or a financial statement.

"Now I know that the one thing you can say about any entrepreneur is that at one point in time they said, 'Screw it. I'm just going to do this.' Even if you think they could have done things differently—or better—you have to give them that. There are lots of people who sit around and say, 'You know what business I think would work . . .' but never do anything about it. That's the difference between an entrepreneur and everybody else."

As someone who's earned a place in the former category, Baker is bullish on the experience. "I was born to do this," he says. "I didn't know that until I did it, but now I know I couldn't work for anyone else."

Mike Moylan, 33
Brendan Moylan, 31

Sports Endeavors

WHAT THEY DO: Produce *Eurosport,*
   Acme Soccer, and *Great Atlantic
   Lacrosse Co.* catalogs
HOME BASE: Hillsborough, North
   Carolina
FOUNDED: 1984
START-UP COSTS: $20,000
1997 SALES: $38 million
1998 PROJECTIONS: $42 million to
   $43 million

When Mike Moylan went away to college, he asked his mom to take care of things while he was gone. Ever the good sport, she agreed—which went way beyond the call of duty. "Most people leave a bowl of fish or a cat or dog when they go to school," Mike says with a laugh. "I left [my mom] a business."

Mike and his brother Brendan launched *Eurosport*, a catalog that offers soccer enthusiasts everything from shin guards to referee uniforms to World Cup trophy key rings, while still in high school. Despite the obvious disadvantages to starting a company at such a young age, the Moylans quickly found that youth had its advantages as well.

Get This Goal

"Inspire, inform, innovate. You're not going to see it laminated on a card; it's just a principle."

—MIKE MOYLAN

"We were not the most sophisticated businesspeople in the world, but we understood the game of soccer," says Brendan. "People let us know right away that there was a market for that." Though their early efforts were not slick, they were sincere—and that allowed the Moylans to develop a devoted following. "There's a lot of authenticity to this business," says Brendan. "And the [soccer world] is still a relatively small community where that kind of thing makes a difference."

Momentum helped, too. "We were in the right place at the right time," says Brendan. "We were able to tap into the explosion of [popularity in] soccer and, at the same time, the growth of the catalog business." The brothers moved into the lacrosse market as a "natural outgrowth" of their soccer business.

If individual inexperience was a handicap, the brothers did find strength in numbers. After 14 years in business together, Mike and Brendan make a pretty formidable team—even if they don't always think in tandem. "In fact," says Brendan, "we're night and day. Everything we look at, we see from opposite perspectives." This may not make for a lot of simple consensus, but it does make the business more rounded. And thankfully, "we've been extremely fortunate that we've always been close."

Ken Wilson, 34

Gatorz LLC

WHAT THEY DO: Manufacture performance sunglasses made from an
aircraft-quality metal alloy
HOME BASE: Poway, California
FOUNDED: 1988
START-UP COSTS: $75
1997 SALES: Over $4 million
1998 PROJECTIONS: $5 million

When Ken Wilson started selling sunglasses, he knew just a little bit about sunglasses—and a lot about bikes. The former motocross racer was working as a sales rep for a motorcycle accessories company. He liked visiting motorcycle shops and communing with the people who worked there, but he wasn't wild about his employers. In fact, he became increasingly disgruntled. "They were so rude, so mean, so jerkish," he recalls. "Finally, one day I said, 'I don't need this anymore. I'm done here.'" And he quit.

There was only one hitch: Wilson was stranded in San Diego, a long way from his hometown of Bowling Green, Kentucky, where he'd sold vacuum cleaners door to door as a student. He had nowhere to go and nothing to go back to. In short, he was stuck.

Rose-Colored Glasses

"If someone had told me at the beginning, 'You know, Ken, here's the deal: Two or three years down the road, you're going to be facing bankruptcy. You're going to have to deal with lawsuits and who knows what else. What do you think?' I don't think I'd be going, 'Oh, great, sign me up.' Sometimes the unknown is good. Once you're there, you can solve the problem, no matter what it is. Now I feel like there's nothing I can't do if I want to."

Wilson went down to the beach to contemplate his predicament. "I didn't know what I was going to do," he says. "I didn't know whether I should go back to Kentucky or try to find another job in California or what. Then I came across this old man selling sunglasses. I asked him some questions about what he was doing, and we got to talking. By the end of our conversation, I said, 'I'm going to sell sunglasses and I'm going to make a lot of money, and I'm never going to treat people the way [my former employer] treated me.'"

He admits he didn't know what he was doing at first. He had never made sunglasses. He had never sold sunglasses. In fact, he doesn't recall even owning a pair of sunglasses prior to starting his company.

But Wilson had a few things going for him. He knew how to sell. And he had a list of contacts at motorcycle shops. Those may not be the first qualities you'd want if you were launching an eyewear business, but they worked for Wilson—not just by default, but by actually providing him with a marketing advantage.

Instead of tackling the competitive mainstream market for sunglasses, Wilson gravitated toward a relatively untapped niche: motorcycle enthusiasts. It was a perfect inroad for an entrepreneur with limited capital and a lot of drive.

From there, Wilson expanded into more mainstream venues. And he kept updating his products, moving from splatter-painted frames to wraparounds to his current brainstorm, sleek glasses made from an aircraft-quality aluminum-and-titanium alloy. Do people really need that kind of durability? "Sure," says Wilson. "People are really rough on their glasses." Besides, 18- to 35-year-olds dig the bulletproof image.

And speaking of bulletproof, perhaps Wilson's latest emphasis on durability springs from his own experience overcoming the odds. "I think the key to my success is my desire to prove everybody who thinks I can't do something wrong," he says. "One thing that's enabled me to pull out of trouble is hearing someone tell me it can't be done. That fires up the adrenaline."

Chapter 7

Do It Better

"A map of the world
that does not
include Utopia
is not worth
even glancing at."

—OSCAR WILDE

Dineh Mohajer, 26
Ben Einstein, 26
Pooneh Mohajer, 33
Hard Candy

WHAT THEY DO: Make and market cosmetics with an attitude, including candy-colored nail polish, lipsticks, eye shadow, and—soon—a full makeup line

HOME BASE: Beverly Hills, California

FOUNDED: 1995

START-UP COSTS: $200

1997 SALES: $10 million

1998 PROJECTIONS: $10 million

Photo© Amy Cantrell

On the day Dineh Mohajer painted her toenails baby blue and went out shoe shopping, starting a business was the last thing on her mind. Mohajer, then 22, was just your basic University of Southern California premed student escaping to Beverly Hills for a mindless summer afternoon of retail therapy with her sister Pooneh.

She wasn't looking for new challenges. *Au contraire*, says Mohajer. "I had decided that summer [in 1995] to blow everything off and do a very unpremed-like thing and just relax before I had to go off to medical school [eventually] and never have another chance to be a kid."

Bring On The Magic Fingers

"I didn't sleep. I didn't eat. I was a working fool. [Finally,] I said, 'I'm hiring a CEO. I'm going to pay him a fat sum of money—all the money I would have made—and let him run everything while I get a massage.'"

—DINEH MOHAJER

She envisioned a summer of partying and kicking back with her boyfriend. What she got was something else. Sporting a shade of polish she had mixed herself, she was accosted by dozens of passersby who simply had to know where she got that polish. A saleswoman at Charles David practically begged Mohajer to reveal her source. The baby blue perfectly complemented Charles David's spring line of shoes.

"That was it," Pooneh recalls. "I told Dineh, 'We're going to lunch and put together a business plan and start selling this stuff.'"

Sell it they did. When Dineh and her boyfriend, Ben Einstein, went to pitch upscale specialty store Fred Segal, an excited teenager ambushed them and insisted on buying the prototypes on the spot. Once Hard Candy nail polish hit the street, *Vogue, Seventeen* and *Elle* turned on the editorial spotlight. Nordstrom, then Bloomingdale's, then Saks called in orders. In a matter of months, the partners were looking at $10 million in annual sales. So much for Dineh's summer of leisure.

In fact, the frenetic pace of Hard Candy's growth took a toll on would-be medical student Dineh, former attorney Pooneh, and musician-turned-marketer Einstein. "Suddenly, people were ordering more than we could possibly make," says Einstein. "We got our friends involved. At one point, we had 12 people working out of a two-room guest house" behind Dineh and Ben's apartment.

And still it wasn't enough. Dineh and Pooneh's mother flew in from Michigan to help. They moved the company into commercial space, found a manufacturer, hired staff. The frenzy continued. Finally, the young partners did the unthinkable: They hired a CEO to whip the company into shape. With the help of William Botts, the three founders have managed to organize the chaos of explosive demand into a working company.

Staying on the cutting edge isn't easy, especially in the cutthroat cosmetics industry. Fortunately, Hard Candy has a visionary at its helm. "Ever since I've known Dineh, she's been able to look at things and say, 'That's cool,' or 'That's cheese,'" says Einstein. "Even in [high] school, she was six months ahead of everyone else."

Some would say she was miles ahead. Before Hard Candy hit the scene, the nail polish industry was as mature as an industry could be—or so it thought. It took three naïve, ambitious, radical-thinking style junkies who didn't know better to shake things up.

Photo© Edward Carreon

Scott Samet, 30
Doug Chu, 30
Taste Of Nature & Tabacon Cigar Co.

WHAT THEY DO: Place and maintain bins of
healthful snack foods at movie theaters
nationwide; market and distribute a
line of cigars and operate a cigar club

HOME BASE: Beverly Hills, California

FOUNDED: Taste of Nature, 1992; Tabacon
Cigar Co., 1994

START-UP COSTS: $20,000

1997 SALES: Taste of Nature, nearly
$2 million; Tabacon Cigar Co.,
$4 million

1998 PROJECTIONS: Taste of Nature, nearly
$4 million; Tabacon Cigar Co.,
$4 million to $5 million

Imagine the horror. You're going to see a movie. You're in the mood for a little snack. You don't like popcorn, and your body isn't up to metabolizing a 50-pound sack of Milk Duds. What will you do? *What will you do?*

Thanks to the work of Scott Samet and Doug Chu, you may still have hope. Their company, Taste of Nature, places bins of alternative snacks—ranging from yogurt-covered pretzels to dried fruit to Oriental party mix—in 800 movie theaters nationwide. Moviegoers bag their own snacks and pay by the weight, so they aren't stuck with the same old popcorn and candy, and they aren't saddled with predetermined portions that would feed the world's ant population for several years.

On With The Show

"When you get a desire to pursue a business that you think has potential, it's very compelling. We knew this was a great idea. And we were young, energetic, eager—which is a great advantage when you're starting a business."

—DOUG CHU

An obvious winner? Maybe to regular folks. But according to Chu and Samet, persuading theater owners to give Taste of Nature a try was about as easy as selling spinach to a 5-year-old. "There was an existing old-boy network [among theater owners] that we were too young to be a part of," says Samet.

"And we were the new kids on the block," says Chu. "That would have been true whether we were 25 or 50. We had to be extremely persistent from a sales perspective."

And flexible, too. Though Taste of Nature originally set out to sell healthful snacks, theater owners soon began asking for candy selections as well. "It wasn't that they didn't want what we were offering," says Chu. "It was that they wanted something more in addition to what we were selling. It meant that we didn't stay true to the healthy niche, but we made the change to accommodate our customers." Ultimately, says Samet, the strategy was to be responsive.

When they saw another opportunity in the marketplace, Chu and Samet launched a cigar division in 1994. The Tabacon Cigar Co.'s ventures include the Monthly Cigar Club and six brands: Tabacon Vintage, Rosa Blanca, Del Valle, Nivelacuso Private Reserve, Don Jivan, and La Diabla.

The cigar business is largely unrelated to Taste of Nature, though the things that made the partners' first project a success have translated well into the second. Among the advantages that Samet and Chu brought to their partnership: learning the ropes at the University of Pennsylvania's Wharton School of Business (where they met), having experience in investment banking (where they were co-workers), and sharing an enthusiasm for entrepreneurship.

Building a $6 million business has been demanding but never demoralizing. "By no means do we want to suggest that we've done everything perfectly, or that we've never made mistakes," says Chu. "You make lots of mistakes, some of which you can control and others you can't. But we've managed to pursue good opportunities and minimize the downside potential so that when something falls flat, we don't lose everything."

Charlie Wilson, 31

SeaRail International

WHAT THEY DO: Buy and sell surplus and damaged products
HOME BASE: Houston
FOUNDED: 1990
START-UP COSTS: $1,000
1997 SALES: $1.3 million
1998 PROJECTIONS: $1.6 million

Photo© Pam Francis

Charlie Wilson was young and idealistic. He wanted to create a world-class business, one that would make him proud. But he was also practical, and his greatest area of expertise—which came from working summers in the family business—was in salvage, buying and selling surplus and damaged goods. Not exactly an industry with a sterling image.

But Wilson didn't let stereotypes stand in the way of pursuing his dream. In 1990, he used the $1,000 his mother gave him as a college graduation gift to launch SeaRail International, a salvage company with a conscience.

Staying Off The Scrap Heap

"Seek advice from people who are already succeeding and surround yourself with people who are smarter than you. Never compromise your ethics. And never quit."

Impossible? Not according to Wilson, who reports that high standards have made all the difference in his company's success. "We're in an industry where a lot of people cut corners. They misrepresent products, minimize damage. In this industry, there's a lot of gray area where we could be less than upfront with customers about the condition of goods," he says. "But you don't get a good reputation this way, and eventually customers don't want to do business with you. We've been able to set ourselves apart by keeping our standards high."

Wilson's interest in excellence doesn't stop at ethics. He's also on a constant campaign to run his business more effectively. For example, after reading Michael E. Gerber's *The E-Myth Revisited*, Wilson reviewed his company's procedures and systems and found ways to improve. "The idea [in the book] is to look at your business as if you're going to franchise it, and to create systems for formulating decisions," he says.

That was but the latest of many instances when Wilson found a way to ratchet up the company's performance by seeking out knowledge. He is an avid reader who readily applies what he learns in business books to his operations.

Wilson is also an inveterate networker, a member of both the Young Entrepreneurs' Organization and the Greater Houston Partnership, the city's equivalent of a chamber of commerce. "Both [organizations] have CEO roundtable programs that have helped me develop as an executive," Wilson reports. "Getting feedback has been extremely helpful when I have major decisions to make."

Also influential: Wilson's mom, a retired systems analyst who is now a full-time painter. "Whenever I've got a tough situation on my hands, I ask myself, 'What would my mother think?' That keeps me honest," says Wilson.

If it sounds as though Wilson's accomplishments can all be attributed to the wisdom of others, consider the character it takes to bring people into the sometimes isolating process of building a business. "When I started this business, I didn't know how an organizational chart should be made. I didn't know how to build a marketing department, how to deal with finances, how to build a sales force. You have to learn to put your ego away and admit that you don't know [something]," says Wilson. "That's the only way to learn to do things right."

Ava DeMarco, 38
Rob Brandegee, 33

Little Earth Productions

WHAT THEY DO: Create fashion accessories made from seat belts, license plates and other recycled goods

HOME BASE: Pittsburgh

FOUNDED: 1993

START-UP COSTS: $10,000

1997 SALES: $3 million

1998 PROJECTIONS: $3 million

When body piercing and black leather just aren't trashy enough, here come Ava DeMarco and Rob Brandegee to save the day. The partners' Little Earth Productions gives trash a good name; it makes belts, bags and accessories from recycled seat belts, license plates, hubcaps and inner tubes.

After seeing similar businesses in action, Brandegee says, he decided to give it a try while he was at the University of Pittsburgh, "desperately trying to finish college." He and DeMarco, a graphic designer, collaborated on the business plan with the help of a course Brandegee took in entrepreneurship. The result? A company whose slick catalog and hip merchandise enjoyed such a strong trade-show presence that even upscale department stores agreed to carry the line.

King Of The Hill

"A marketing consultant told us once that if you're going to start a business, you want to be a dominant player in your industry—No. 1, 2 or 3. If you're not, you need to narrow your niche until you can be a dominant player. That advice has helped us focus on where the company should be."

—AVA DEMARCO

The key, according to DeMarco, was the right combination of trend-surfing and trend-setting. "Other companies were doing [recycled] products, but they weren't really being promoted as cool," she explains. "We thought if we could make products that were cool first—and also [capitalize on] the recycling trend—it would be really easy to sell them."

They were right. Little Earth products have virtually sold themselves. *Making* the products, on the other hand, has presented some challenges. "Probably the hardest part of our start-up was finding the recycled materials to work with," says DeMarco. "We used to literally drive around to landfills and junkyards, collecting materials." Now, Little Earth deals with a network of unique suppliers (seven used license plate dealers, for example), who are in turn enjoying a renaissance thanks to the company's success.

DeMarco and Brandegee had the good fortune to catch the recycling wave when it hit. But they've also had the good sense to keep innovating as that trend has cycled in and out. "We're depending more on diversification now," reports DeMarco. "We're doing custom products for corporations, for example. And we're bringing prices down through manufacturing efficiencies."

Turning heads in the fashion world has been fun for the partners, but that's only part of the picture. For DeMarco, the big reward is running an environmentally friendly company. And Brandegee says he's most gratified to be improving their employees' quality of life. "Ideas are really cheap," says DeMarco. "It's going out and doing it that makes a difference." Nothing trashy about that.

Brett Kingstone, 39

Super Vision International Inc.

WHAT THEY DO: Manufacture fiber optic lighting cable that's an unbreakable alternative to neon

HOME BASE: Orlando, Florida

FOUNDED: 1990

START-UP COSTS: $100,000

1997 SALES: $9.2 million

1998 PROJECTIONS: $15 million

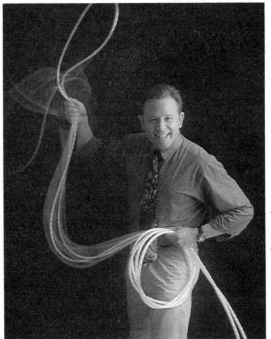

Photo© Dimensions Photography

Brett Kingstone didn't start out with much. At 19, he began assembling parts for his first fiber optic business on the dining room table in his Stanford University dorm room. "Then I graduated to a garage," he says.

There were setbacks. His first company went out of business as the result of a legal battle with a giant corporation. "In the end, they could spend more money in court than we could," says Kingstone, who went on to found what is now Super Vision International.

What allowed Kingstone to prevail? He may not have had much, but he had a good idea—specifically, the patents to a technology that could ultimately overtake the multi-billion-dollar neon industry. Kingstone's proprietary fiber optic lighting cable mimics neon at one-third the energy consumption. And it's unbreakable. "Fiber optics [have] none of the maintenance and disposal problems [of neon]: no glass, no high voltage," he says.

Read All About It

I'd advise [aspiring entrepreneurs] to go out and buy all the books they can find by successful entrepreneurs—especially in the industry they're interested in. You can spend $24.95 and a weekend of your time doing that, or go through the rest of your life living the same mistakes."

That's good enough to fuel 1,000 percent sales growth at Super Vision over the past four years. It's good enough to light up Times Square, with a giant Coca-Cola bottle as well as an AT&T sign so gargantuan that the fiber in it, stretched out, would reach more than halfway from Manhattan to Orlando.

And still it's not quite good enough for Kingstone, who says his company's potential has only begun to be tapped. "A lot of people ask me, 'When will you say you're a success?'" he says. "On the sales side, it's when our sales become a certain percentage of the overall neon market; on the earnings side, it's when every employee in this company—including the receptionist and the people on the production line—can pay off their mortgages and put their kids through college."

Kingstone knows how they'll get there, too. "It's [going to take] sheer, dogged determination," he says, "and the dedication to make it happen. I guess we may have come close to the edge over the years, but we've willed it never to happen. That's how we get where we're going. We could be selling any product and it wouldn't make any difference. It's the passion and the will."

Peter Siegel, 30
Bob Spiegel, 37
Carla Ruben, 36

Daily Soup

WHAT THEY DO: Sell soup, beautiful soup, in a fast format at nine locations

HOME BASE: New York City

FOUNDED: 1996

START-UP COSTS: $225,000

1997 SALES: $7 million

1998 PROJECTIONS: $10 million to $11 million

Not since Campbell's put the stuff in cans has soup been such hot stuff. We're not talking about the greasy, watery liquid that passes for soup in most affordable eateries. We're talking about spicy Moroccan chicken or Thai chilled melon with peanuts. This is soup you can live on.

"We're taking something that's been around for hundreds of years and redefining it," says Carla Ruben, co-founder of the Daily Soup chain. "We're making [soup] more of a meal. We try to imagine the customer taking the soup and putting it on a piece of bread and making it a sandwich."

A Lot To Swallow

"The impression that you're working for yourself when you're in a business like this is wrong. You're working for your employees—and your customers—not just a boss. It's that many more people you have to answer to."

—BOB SPIEGEL

Revolutionary? Only when you consider the scarcity of fast, nutritional, satisfying options for lunch, or even a quick post-workout dinner.

Ruben and partners Bob Spiegel and Peter Siegel knew from the beginning they were onto something. But it wasn't until the month they opened that they got their first premonition of a landslide. The "Soup Nazi" episode of "Seinfeld" ran two weeks before Daily Soup opened its doors. In it, New Yorkers clamor for bowls of broth and bisque from a regulation-obsessed and cranky (but ingenious) soup vendor.

Two weeks later, life imitated art—minus the surly chef. "After our second day, we had hundreds and hundreds of people lining the streets for our soup," says Ruben. "We knew we would be successful, but we didn't expect that."

Since then, it's been one great bowl after another. The partners stress that theirs is not a whimsical business. Before launching Daily Soup, Spiegel and Ruben had their own catering company, so food service was not new to the trio. And from the start, a chain of restaurants was the ultimate goal.

"From there, the challenge was opening a store with the knowledge that we would be opening more," says Ruben. "We paid a lot of attention to the systems we were creating. We developed a very strong identity," which is expressed in everything from store graphics to employee training and in-store music.

For all the brainpower that went into the concept, the partners found plenty of joy in producing a new venture. "We all really, really enjoyed setting the business up," says Spiegel. "It was completely creative. Any idea you came up with, you could implement in the beginning. There was no bureaucracy, nothing to stop you from doing what you wanted."

What do the partners want now? Expansion beyond Manhattan is next on the menu. In time, says Ruben, the plan is "definitely" to go nationwide. "We've got 500 different types of soups, and they're all delicious," says Ruben. "We just keep getting bigger and better."

Chapter 8

Attitude Adjustment

> "Since the house is on fire, let us warm ourselves."
>
> —ITALIAN PROVERB

David Morris, 31
Chris Heyer, 23

Dillanos Coffee Roasters

WHAT THEY DO: Wholesale coffee
HOME BASE: Sumner, Washington
FOUNDED: 1990
START-UP COSTS: $35,000
1997 SALES: $2 million
1998 PROJECTIONS: About $3.5 million

Photo© Hot Shots/Dale Barber

David Morris will tell you that the vehicle is never as important as the driver. He should know. Early in his life, Morris was a professional bicycle stunt rider. On the side, he conducted motivational assemblies at schools. It was a good life, but, as Morris observes, "You can't ride a bike into your 40s."

So he bought a little espresso cart—back in the days when espresso was still somewhat of a novelty—and stationed himself outside a local convenience store. Morris made it his business to learn the name and order of every regular customer. His enterprise might have been small, but it wasn't going to be insignificant.

Sip By Sip

"It's not enough to think you're going to enjoy the money. When you're starting a business, it may take years to reach the goal of financial independence. If you're not having fun during all those years, you're missing the point."

—DAVID MORRIS

The business thrived, but Morris felt a chill—literally. "I was out there at 5:30 in the morning. It was cold," he recalls. So he arranged to station his cart inside. And he decided to bring his brother, Chris Heyer, on board with a second cart and an offer of partnership. More carts followed. Soon, Morris and Heyer had a whole fleet.

But they weren't alone. Dillanos found itself in the midst of a coffee extravaganza. Washington had become *latte* nation. There were coffee stores and coffeehouses, coffee drive-thrus and coffee bars. Suddenly, peddling espresso was a hot idea—so hot that even dry cleaners and Laundromats were getting in on the action.

Meanwhile, Heyer and Morris spotted an intriguing opportunity. "Our coffee roaster was supplying us with good coffee and good service, but we thought they should have been giving us even better coffee and even better service," says Morris. "After all, the more espresso we served, the more money we both would make." Realizing that other retailers and coffee bars might feel likewise, Morris and Heyer began roasting and wholesaling their own beans.

It was kismet. Heyer and Morris were good retailers, but they're exceptional wholesalers. Morris' creative and marketing skills, teamed with Heyer's organizational talents, deliver what few competitors can. Theirs is a wholesale business that's conscientious enough to offer marketing kits and color-customized point-of-sale materials to its clients, and efficient enough to make ideas like those work.

Customer service is so important that Morris and Heyer plant tape recorders in their delivery trucks so that drivers can record random observations about clients as they make their stops. "Every Monday morning from 7 to 9:30, we all sit down and listen to those tapes and talk about what we can do to address our customers' concerns," says Morris. "It's helped us serve our customers better, and it's a great marketing tool to be able to tell potential customers that we do this."

Dillanos' wholesale division has been so successful that its retail carts are history. Heyer and Morris are glad to have been cart operators; the experience enlightens their wholesale efforts. But they're also happy to be where they are now. Wheels or no wheels, the driver's seat is the place to be.

Richard Swerdlow, 34
Andres Link, 31

Everything Wireless

WHAT THEY DO: Sell wireless accessories through catalogs, the Internet and five retail locations

HOME BASE: Hollywood, Florida

FOUNDED: 1993

START-UP COSTS: $18,000

1997 SALES: About $9 million

1998 PROJECTIONS: $12 million

They had a fine idea. Corporate lawyer Richard Swerdlow and his friend Andres Link, a banker, thought they would sell cellular phone service from a mall kiosk. But that would have placed them in direct competition with another phone store in the mall, and that was against mall policy. So Link and Swerdlow switched to selling cellular phone accessories under the name Cellular Works.

Call it a $9 million accident. Five years later the company, now called Everything Wireless, is one of the premier sources of wireless accessories anywhere. Gadgets include hands-free kits for mobile phone users and data devices that let you use wireless communication to retrieve e-mail and send files. With wireless technology growing faster than light travels down a fiber optic cable—and consumers buying it just as fast—Swerdlow and Link couldn't be in a more enviable position.

On The Line

"Don't underestimate the amount of capital you need to build a business. If you have a good idea with a lot of potential, you're going to need money to achieve your goals."

—RICHARD SWERDLOW

Of course, getting here wasn't hands-free. The formula for success: "Stick-to-it-iveness," says Link. That, and the determination to stay ahead of emerging trends in technology—in the company's product mix and in its marketing.

For example, Everything Wireless was among the first companies in the industry to put up a Web page. "We've been on the Internet since 1993," says Swerdlow. "[The Web site] Internet Shopper named us the granddaddy of wireless communications companies on the Web."

Swerdlow and Link have also been aggressive about finding the right channels for their products. In addition to the Web site, catalog and retail stores, Everything Wireless makes its products available through the in-flight catalog *Sky Mall.*

Growing so large was no easy feat for two guys who started out with a mere $18,000. The biggest challenge, according to Swerdlow, has been managing people. "Entrepreneurs are traditionally good at making deals," he says. "But when you have a growing company, you also have to manage a staff—and you don't necessarily have the capital to hire midlevel managers to whom you can delegate some of that responsibility."

To aspiring entrepreneurs, Swerdlow telegraphs this message: "Find a niche and stay focused on it. Entrepreneurs have a lot of good ideas, but you have to resist pursuing all of them and just focus on the one you think has the most potential."

Alan Greenwood, 39
Cleo Greenwood, 37

Vintage Guitar Inc.

> **WHAT THEY DO:** Publish a monthly tabloid magazine for vintage guitar collectors
>
> **HOME BASE:** Bismarck, North Dakota
>
> **FOUNDED:** 1986
>
> **START-UP COSTS:** $2,500
>
> **1997 SALES:** $1.5 million
>
> **1998 PROJECTIONS:** $1.7 million

"Some people collect salt-and-pepper shakers. Our readers collect guitars," says Alan Greenwood of the audience for his monthly magazine, *Vintage Guitar*. It seems vintage six-strings are back by popular demand among baby boomers who saw the Beatles play on "Ed Sullivan," young music buffs who want a slice of music history, and even some of today's most popular musicians.

Alan and his wife, Cleo, can speak authoritatively about the market now. But 12 years ago, when the Greenwoods jumped into the publishing business, they weren't quite as in tune with their readership as they are today.

"This was supposed to be an upper Midwest regional shopper; it was originally called *The Music Trader*," says Cleo. "But people began calling us and saying, 'You should talk to this person,' or 'Why don't you write about this?'" Slowly, the focus changed from the general marketplace for used musical instruments to the specific interests of guitar aficionados.

Living Amplified

"The biggest challenge is all the stress, all the time. We gamble every day by taking out an ad or changing our distributor. Even growth is stressful. In fact, growth spurts seem like the hardest, trying to keep up with day-to-day operations and think about the future. It's great having a [successful] company, but it's not easy."

—CLEO GREENWOOD

Packed with product details, artist profiles, company histories, and book and music reviews, the magazine clearly strikes a chord; some 42,000 readers tune in to *Vintage Guitar* each month. No one's more pleased—or surprised—by its success than the Greenwoods.

"At first we thought, 'If the magazine could support us

both part time, that would be great,'" recalls Cleo. "Then we thought, 'If it could support one of us full time . . .' Then we were happy it was supporting us both. Now, we've got a full staff and we're continuing to grow."

"It's doing what I expected it to do, but it's gone beyond what I dreamed it would do," quips Alan.

Keeping the harmony while building a business—and a family—has taken some discipline. "We've had to learn to turn off being businesspeople when we go home, because it stresses the kids out when we talk about work," Cleo says of their three young children. "We've made a rule to try not to talk about business after 8 o'clock. But it's hard. Sometimes we stop in midsentence. I'll run upstairs and make a note and bring the notes to the office the next day."

Marc Levy, 31
Spence Levy, 28
Jay Abramowitz, 31

Café Cola

WHAT THEY DO: Bottle and distribute a
coffee-flavored cola drink
HOME BASE: Miami Beach, Florida
FOUNDED: 1995
START-UP COSTS: $80,000
1997 SALES: $1 million
1998 PROJECTIONS: $1.5 million

Pulling all-nighters during finals is the norm for most college students. But brothers Marc and Spence Levy and their buddy Jay Abramowitz, self-proclaimed caffeine junkies, didn't just hit the books during late-night cram sessions—they also threw together homemade cola-and-coffee concoctions for the ultimate caffeine rush.

After college the three made their way into corporate America, but the working world didn't offer much of a jolt. Marc joined the family manufacturing business. Abramowitz had his own finance company. "I had a job in sales, and I was making a lot of money for my boss," says Spence. "Finally, I said, 'Why shouldn't I be making this money for myself?' I asked my brother and Jay if they'd like to start a business together, and they said yes."

They'll Drink To That

"Until I quit my job in May 1995—a whole year after we started the company—we were literally working all day at our jobs and then 15 or 16 hours a day on Café Cola. That's where our product came in handy, though. [The caffeine] let us stay up and do the work."

—SPENCE LEVY

But what kind of business? Maybe it was nostalgia. Or maybe a late-night brainstorming session prompted the trio to mix up a batch of coffee colas for old times' sake. Either way, the partners were soon taste-testing combinations of coffee and cola in hopes of finding that perfect formula.

They did it. Impossible as it may sound, they created a drink made of coffee and cola that actually tastes good. The battle was won.

But the war was just beginning. "It's not easy to get shelf space [in U.S. stores]," says Abramowitz. "You have to have a proven sales record, and that's impossible for a new company." In fact, beverage distribution channels were so tight that Café Cola almost ran out of juice. Though the product is sold through more than 240 stores in South Florida, and has made inroads in Minnesota, nationwide distribution has been elusive.

That's where ingenuity (or perhaps the benefit of excess caffeine) has come in handy. Frustrated by barriers in the U.S. market, the partners decided to launch Café Cola overseas. The result: The company exports some 90 percent of its product to Argentina, Brazil, Denmark, El Salvador, Sri Lanka, Singapore and the Bahamas.

Not only are barriers to entry lower in other countries, but marketing is also a relative breeze. "Here, you walk into a convenience store and face a wall of beverages to choose from," says Spence. "In other countries, the selection might be half of what it is here." Overseas, American products have a special cachet, which gives Café Cola a marketing edge.

The partners still aspire to expand Café Cola's distribution in the United States. But meanwhile, they're pleased with the reception they're getting abroad—and the opportunity it's providing for them to keep their dream alive.

"We've been up against failure many times," says Spence. "Many times it's gotten so bad that I feel grateful we can laugh about it now. But somehow, at the last minute, something has always worked out. On the other hand, the reason things have always worked out is that we never stop working."

Mitch Cahn, 31

Headcase

WHAT THEY DO: Manufacture clothing
and headwear "fortified" with
hemp, and customized baseball
caps

HOME BASE: Jersey City, New Jersey

FOUNDED: 1992

START-UP COSTS: $35,000

1997 SALES: $2.6 million

1998 PROJECTIONS: $3.5 million

Photo© John Emerson

154

Mitch Cahn didn't mean to become an advocate for hemp. He was just a guy who wanted to make baseball caps. The former Wall Street financial analyst headed into the business after his father tipped him off to an auction sale of a defunct cap company. "It was an opportunity to buy [a business] at a low investment, so that if it didn't work out, I wouldn't lose much," says Cahn.

But a baseball cap is a baseball cap is a baseball cap . . . without a gimmick, at least. "I had to find a way to market the product that was new," says Cahn. The answer: Adding hemp—a strong, natural, environmentally friendly fiber that's related to, but not the same as, marijuana.

Head And Shoulders

" I always knew I didn't want to work for anyone. I just didn't know whether or not that included myself. Now, I think I'm a pretty good boss."

Although controversial, hemp is indisputably practical. "It's the most durable fiber there is," says Cahn. "And it's much more sustainable than cotton. It can be grown without pesticides anywhere. It's a weed." Headcase's "hemp-fortified" caps and clothing are not only tougher, thanks to their hemp content, but they also feature what Cahn calls "subtly subversive" messages such as "Warning: Do Not Smoke This Cap" and "Hemp Wanted."

Cahn was fortunate enough to catch the hemp trend at the right time. When he started, competition was sparse and revenues grew like—well, weeds. Soon, Headcase hats and clothes were available in eco-stores and clothing boutiques around the world. But over time, competition in the hemp marketplace grew, and Cahn began casting about for an additional niche.

"We were losing business to companies that make hats overseas, so I tried to think of new markets—markets that wouldn't buy from overseas companies," he says. "When I asked myself which markets those might be, I came up with labor unions."

Bingo. As it turns out, says Cahn, "Labor unions buy a lot of baseball caps. And they definitely don't want to buy goods from overseas." Today, caps for labor unions make up about half the company's sales.

For Cahn, entrepreneurship is a heads-up experience. "We're always looking for new directions," he says. "It's a constant storm." Yet he wonders "If I was living in Vermont and working at a video store, would these thoughts go away?"

Robert Dobrient, 37

Max Distribution/Dynamex

WHAT THEY DO: Same-day transportation and distribution

HOME BASE: Dallas and Irving, Texas

FOUNDED: 1985

START-UP COSTS: None

1997 SALES: About $9 million

1998 PROJECTIONS: $11 million

In 1996, Robert Dobrient faced a wrenching choice: Finance a buyout of his estranged partner or sell the company he had spent 11 years building. Like any entrepreneur, he wanted to keep his business. He'd taken Max Distribution from a two-person enterprise—running on little more than a pair of funky cars, a college dorm room and the energy of two eager students—to a multimillion-dollar operation growing at roughly 40 percent per year.

Not Made In Heaven

"You should be married to one person in life—your spouse. If you're thinking about going into partnership with someone, do it with a clearly defined exit strategy, so that the process of breaking up the partnership doesn't mean the end of your business. Build in an arbitration mechanism. Or think about hiring the expertise that a partner might bring to the table instead. You're risking a lot when you gamble on a [partner relationship] surviving as long as your business does."

But when he calculated the cost of buying out his partner, Dobrient saw there was a high price to pay for maintaining ownership. "Basically, I couldn't stand the thought of holding the company back for two years just for the sake of preserving my position," he says. "Also, I could see that the industry was consolidating." In the end, he chose to sell Max Distribution to Irving, Texas-based Dynamex so that the business he had worked so hard to establish could continue thriving even as its founding partnership dissolved.

It's a decision Dobrient is still living with—happily. As vice president of marketing and business development for Dynamex, he says, "I have a senior management position at a company that we think is positioned to become the leader in same-day package delivery, just as FedEx is the leader in next-day. It's a new level of pressure working here, but I'm also learning more than I ever have."

As for the company, "It's actually performing better than it ever has," reports Dobrient. "Recently, I brought someone through the facility and they said, in an environment as busy as that, to see so many people smiling but still focused on their work is incredible. That felt good."

At 37, Dobrient isn't unique among senior-level executives; others have reached similar points at similar ages. But the route Dobrient took is extraordinary. In a flash, he is back in his Volkswagen Rabbit transporting packages, wondering what the next day's business might deliver.

"Looking back, doing all of this when I was young was a huge advantage," he says. "I did it when I could afford to make mistakes. No mistake could finish me off. In some ways that was because I wasn't smart enough to know when to quit, but I also had nothing to lose. I was 23 and I owned a $1,200 car. What could I possibly lose?"

Thirteen years, one acquisition, and millions of dollars later, Dobrient may have more on the line, but he still has his eyes on the prize. Only the eyes and the prizes have changed.

Chapter 9

Never Say Die

"When you get into a
tight place and everything
goes against you, till it seems
as though you could not
hang on a minute longer,
never give up then,
for that is just the place
and time that
the tide will turn."

—HARRIET BEECHER STOWE

Gina Ellis, 37
Bill Ellis, 40
Quatrine Washable Furniture

WHAT THEY DO: Retail and manufacture
European-style sofas and chairs
with washable slipcovers; seven
locations nationwide
HOME BASE: Torrance, California
FOUNDED: 1990
START-UP COSTS: $40,000
1997 SALES: Over $5 million
1998 PROJECTIONS: $10 million

Photo© *Los Angeles Times*/Genaro Molina

Gina Ellis had the vision. She wasn't a furniture maker, but she knew what she wanted: comfortable, slipcovered sofas and chairs like the ones she had known while living in Spain. In Southern California, however, no such furniture existed.

That was how she found herself in East Los Angeles, negotiating with an upholsterer to get just the right oversized, European-style, loosely covered pieces she wanted. And, bravo—they were brilliant. Friends were so bowled over that they asked Gina to get similar pieces for them.

Pillow Talk

"You can become too informed [in business]. It's easy to get inundated with all this information that's out there, and you start second-guessing what people want."

—BILL ELLIS

"The experts tell us every day what we're supposed to be doing, but all they're doing all day is researching. We're standing right there when the customer places an order. We never lose sight of our customer relationships—and that's where our strength lies."

—GINA ELLIS

What made the sofa and chairs so fabulous? Hip styling, comfort, and—thanks to the slipcovers—washability. No matter what life threw at it, the furniture was always but a machine washing away from renewal.

How fitting, then, that the same furniture became the centerpiece of a new business for Gina and her husband, Bill—not only because they, too, are stylish and smart, but because life has put them through plenty of wear and tear.

It began in 1989 when, five days before Christmas, Bill lost his job as associate creative director for an advertising agency. The couple's first child was on her way, and their mortgage was so new that they hadn't made their first payment yet. Meanwhile, Gina's job as a retail buyer was also less than satisfying.

In true Ellis style, Gina and Bill didn't implode; they started thinking. If the furniture was so popular with their friends, wasn't it possible that others would like it, too? True, being unemployed and tending a newborn don't usually go hand-in-hand with starting a business. But then, wasn't this precisely the kind of situation that cried out for action?

Act they did. Using $40,000 in equity from their newly purchased home, they launched Quatrine from a tiny shop in the Los Angeles suburb of Manhattan Beach. It was not an immediate hit. Display pieces—which included five new pieces and three from the Ellises' living room—drew raves from curious passersby, but were so expensive that they didn't sell.

Just as Bill and Gina were wondering how they could continue, they made a $14,000 sale—enough to keep the doors open and give them the breathing room they needed to regroup. They streamlined their offerings and, in the process, were able to cut prices almost in half. It was the beginning of commercial viability.

But it wasn't the end of the story. Three years later, Quatrine was holding its own, but the prognosis for Los Angeles wasn't great. "The economy was in a slump and the riots had just happened," Bill recalls. "Gina and I were living a very modest lifestyle," thanks to the area's astronomical cost of living. "We flew out to Michigan for a wedding, and by the time we came back, we had agreed to open a second store there."

The Quatrine in Birmingham, Michigan, was a success from day one. The Ellises bought a lakefront home in precisely the kind of picturesque, eclectic community they'd always dreamed of.

The story doesn't end there, either. "Our business grew to the point that we needed to be in L.A., where all the manufacturing was," says Gina. "I remember looking at Bill and saying, 'You know what? We aren't here yet. We aren't at the place where we can run our lives from the house next to the lake.'"

So they moved back. And they grew the business, expanding into Chicago, Houston, Dallas, Denver, and a second L.A. suburb, Redondo Beach. They recently added manufacturing to the mix, and they're looking to move into the San Francisco Bay area, Atlanta and possibly Las Vegas. With the Ellises' knockout products, knack for design, and innate durability, and a little luck, sales should approach $10 million in 1998.

And if the road getting here hasn't been a straight line, that's fine with Bill and Gina. They're prepared to handle the chills and spills of an action-packed entrepreneurial life. They even have the slipcovers to prove it.

Dino Miliotis, 33

Bug-Ban

WHAT THEY DO: Distribute Bug-Ban, a nontoxic, mosquito-repellent wristband sold worldwide

HOME BASE: Wood Dale, Illinois

FOUNDED: 1996

START-UP COSTS: $25

1997 SALES: $18 million

1998 PROJECTIONS: $30 million

Past flops don't bug Dino Miliotis. He'll tell you all about the time he put together a door-to-door marketing force for hire. Or about trying to sell limited-edition artwork from an artist's unheated studio. Or about the collector plate business that didn't take off, or the sports memorabilia business that did—and then fizzled. Miliotis estimates he had seven "harebrained schemes" that got away before he finally found an idea that bit.

Even Miliotis' success story wasn't a case of love at first sight. "To be truthful, I wasn't that excited about [Bug-Ban]," he says. "But I got in touch with some of my contacts and they immediately saw the applications. They called me and said, 'I was up all night thinking about this . . .'"

Buzzed

In this kind of business, when people call you, you have to be alert and ready to make decisions that may be worth millions of dollars. It's easy to get overwhelmed, so I don't like leaving anything to chance. I never leave the office today without knowing what I'm doing tomorrow. On Monday, I set a target for the week; on Friday, I have closure. That's the only way to stay on top. We don't throw darts here."

So it was that Miliotis was bitten by the entrepreneurial bug—again, and this time for good. Bug-Ban—the brainchild of Miliotis' friend Bill Canale (who now owns and operates DPM Enterprises' manufacturing division)—is an adjustable plastic wristband. It snaps on (not unlike a flea collar) and provides up to 40 hours of protection against mosquitoes. The plastic contains naturally fragrant lemongrass oil, citronella and geranium oil. It works without toxic chemicals or any mess, and comes with a special vapor-barrier bag that preserves its potency when not in use.

What makes it a hit? One answer is its range of appeal. For instance, golfers prefer it to sticky sprays that can interfere with their grip. Natural food store shoppers are also fans, because Bug-Ban is nontoxic.

From another perspective, Bug-Ban's success can be directly attributed to the buzz of energy that is Miliotis. His start-up capital was so meager that he had to borrow a cubicle from which to work. "I had one phone with call waiting, and it was constantly ringing," says Miliotis. "I was two-finger typing all the invoices myself. I sent out 1,200 information packets a week."

Miliotis worked his way into major retail accounts like Wal-Mart and Home Depot with the help of a strong network—mainly people he met in his previous business incarnations. "I'm building this company on rapport and circles of influence," he says. "You've got to understand that the poor buyers of this world aren't sitting around at their desks, making necklaces out of paper clips, waiting for you to call. They've got to look at 1,000 to 100,000 new product lines annually. So when little Dino Miliotis sends them a packet, how do they differentiate me from anyone else? Without contacts, it's tough."

You might say Miliotis' action-packed past was just preparation for his current success. Though he laughs about the roller-coaster ride that was his early career, he's also grateful to have had it. "You get to find yourself while you're doing these things," he says. "I'd tell anyone with a good idea, don't stop trying. You may be missing something—age or experience—but with experience, you can learn."

Photo© Chris Arend

Ron Perry, 36

Microware Computers

WHAT THEY DO: Systems integration, including computer networking, telephony and system upgrades

HOME BASE: Anchorage, Alaska

FOUNDED: 1990

START-UP COSTS: $1,200

1997 SALES: $3 million

1998 PROJECTIONS: $2.5 million to $3.5 million

Ron Perry didn't start his own business to satisfy his ego. He did it to make money—not because he's in love with cash but because a difficult divorce left him broke and in peril of losing a custody battle for his daughter. "The idea of [my ex-wife] taking my daughter away from me was unbearable," says Perry. "I knew I needed to make more money." He'd been a successful salesperson for a computer company. Now, he knew, it was time to strike out on his own.

But what a time it was. "I had nothing but $1,200 left on a credit card," Perry recalls. The only way he had a chance was to move in with his parents, whose home was in the process of being built. "I said, 'Let me make you a deal: If the business works, I'll finish [paying off] the house for you,'" Perry says. Then he went to work.

"You'd be surprised what starving will motivate you to do," jokes Perry.

Hard Drive

"**Y**ou never take a look at what's against you. You don't say, 'There are 70 other companies out there.' You put your blinders on and do it."

It took every ounce of salesmanship he had to get Microware going. His pitch: "I'm the guy who's been fixing your computer; I'm the guy you've been calling whenever you have a problem. I'm the same guy you know, only now I'm doing this for myself." And by the way, if clients wanted to continue working with Perry, they had to pay upfront because he didn't have the capital to float them.

Amazingly, clients went for it. "People can sense when you're honest," says Perry, though he also admits that the commitment certainly hasn't been one-sided. One Christmas Eve, Perry went so far as to make a house call to help get a screen saver working. "For me, that's part of doing the job," he says.

Today, Microware and its 12 staffers are flourishing. In addition to installing computer systems and training users on applications, Microware is adding wireless Internet services to its offerings this year.

Equally important, Perry and his family are doing much better, thank you. Over the first three or four years of Microware's growth, he made good on his promise to complete his parents' home. When construction was finished, "I furnished [the house]," says Perry. "Then we put in the lawn, put the fence up, paved the driveway—and on the day they finished the driveway, I moved out." Perry also won custody of his daughter, which makes the happy ending complete.

In retrospect, even Perry isn't sure how he managed to accomplish everything he has, except to say this: "If you have the desire and the will, you can do it. You have to do it long and hard, but you can get there."

Jeff Thompson, 28

Peripheral Enhancements Corp.

WHAT THEY DO: Design, manufacture and distribute computer memory upgrade products

HOME BASE: Ada, Oklahoma

FOUNDED: 1987

START-UP COSTS: $2,500

1997 SALES: $42 million

1998 PROJECTIONS: $80 million

Photo Courtesy: Peripheral Enhancements Corp.

Most people look back on their college days and re-member football games and tough term papers. Jeff Thompson recalls sitting in his apartment fuming while the computer company he'd started in high school operated 60 miles away. "Deals were being made and I couldn't be there to see it all happen," he laments.

Such is the plight of an entrepreneur who launched his first business at the age of 16. "I got into this as a hobby, buying and selling used computer systems as a kid," Thompson explains. "In 1990, I saw an opportunity in computer memory upgrades, so I started focusing on that."

Memory? What Memory?

"[B]eing young,] my mind wasn't cluttered with a lot of ideas about how you run a company. I had never experienced corporate politics; my thinking wasn't adulterated with knowledge of how other companies do things, so I just did things the way they made the most sense to me."

As focused as you can be, that is, when you're also at-tending high school all day. "It was extremely tough to manage my time and keep my focus where it had to be while I was in school," says Thompson. He and two em-ployees worked out of his parents' home until 1989, when he went off to the University of Oklahoma and—as he puts it—"continued micromanaging as I always had" with the help of a dedicated computer link.

"After I graduated, I suddenly had all this time to devote to the company," Thompson says. "That's when I realized how difficult it had been to handle school and [entrepre-neurship] at the same time."

That's one of many excuses that have passed Thompson by. His age and his commitment to school should have sidelined him. Inexperience certainly wasn't any picnic.

"This is a very fast-paced business," says Thompson. "I learned the hard way that keeping one's word didn't mean the same thing to other people that it did to me."

More recently, a precipitous drop in computer memory prices could have proved fatal. "Our pricing has fallen 97 percent in two years," says Thompson. "That means, literally, that a product we sold for $1,000 two years ago now sells for $30."

How do you deal with a curve ball like that? In some ways, Thompson's job has become more like a stockbroker's than a traditional entrepreneur's. "It's more important than ever that we manage our stock," he says. "We keep no more than a couple of days' inventory at a time because the price of a part might drop overnight. You have to live in the here and now."

And you need the tenacity to keep swinging. "You've just got to be stubborn enough—or stupid enough—to keep trying," says Thompson.

Michael Harris, 30
Gregg Garnick, 35

Quadrant International

WHAT THEY DO: Manufacture digital
video peripherals for desktop and
laptop computers

HOME BASE: Bala Cynwyd, Pennsylvania

FOUNDED: 1994

START-UP COSTS: $150,000

1997 SALES: $8.5 million

1998 PROJECTIONS: Over $20 million

Gregg Garnick co-founded a $32 million computer peripherals company, Great Valley Products, then watched as sales of Amiga computers—the platform on which Great Valley was based—foundered and finally fizzled. "We took Great Valley Products from $0 and running from my apartment to $32 million in four years, developing peripherals for the Commodore and Amiga platforms," Garnick says. When Amiga disappeared from the personal computing scene in 1995, Great Valley's business all but evaporated overnight. It was not the ending Garnick had in mind.

So he started over—new beginning, new story, and hopefully a different ending. With co-founder Michael Harris, Garnick has constructed Quadrant International, a company that's bringing digital video to computer systems around the world.

How does a small high-tech company get its products into a competitive marketplace? For Harris and Garnick, the answer is persistence, persistence and more persistence.

Get The Picture

"I would classify myself as a lucky person, but I also think you make your own luck. People see what we've done, and they think we're lucky. They don't see the late-night dinners and the late-night phone calls."

—GREGG GARNICK

The two launched Quadrant International with $150,000 and one product—a board that enables users to bring video to their laptop computers. Now people can plug into their home computers and edit videotape.

To make inroads in an industry dominated by giant companies, Garnick and Harris have adopted a never-say-die attitude. "The selling game is endless," explains Garnick. "You have to sell the bank, your customers, the suppliers—everybody from your landlord to the guy selling you boxes. You even have to sell [potential employees] to come on board."Though Quadrant International is a small player in a big field, its aspirations are anything but modest. "We have the ability to develop the standard for video on PCs," says Garnick. "The question is, how can we set those standards?"

One way is by hiring hot technical talent—not an easy thing to do in a crowded labor market. Here, says Garnick, being young has been an advantage. "We've been able to foster great relationships with people in our same age bracket," he reports. "They're willing to belly up—at least for a time—because they like what we're doing."

And employees aren't the only ones who feel that way. Quadrant International just secured $18 million in financing to help fuel expansion. Winning that kind of confidence requires solid business skills. But youthful exuberance hasn't hurt, either. "People like our enthusiasm," says Garnick. "We're young, aggressive guys trying to build a company. People respond to that."

Mark Lee, 39
Jeff McCarty, 33

The Original Time Capsule Company

WHAT THEY DO: Design and manufacture time capsule kits for new
parents, newlyweds and new
graduates
HOME BASE: Greenfield, Indiana
FOUNDED: 1992
START-UP COSTS: $65,000
1997 SALES: $1.5 million
1998 PROJECTIONS: $2.2 million

Jeff McCarty must have been put on earth to help people preserve their memories. How else do you explain his peculiar story? Smack in the middle of a promising career in graphic design, McCarty quit his job to work full time on what he intuited was his life's work: Creating "time capsule" kits to help people commemorate important events in their lives.

"My entire life, I had been stashing away memorabilia in boxes and collecting pop culture items from my birth year," says McCarty. "To me, it was absolutely fascinating how much daily life in America had changed in a relatively short period of time." When it occurred to him that he could create a product to help others collect their own memories, he was so excited and moved by the possibility that he became misty-eyed talking about it.

Taking The Time

"I read once that the average person comes up with four ideas per year that would make them a millionaire, but most don't do anything about them. Now that I've been through it, I know that you start out not knowing how much of your time and personal resources it's really going to take. But [getting through it] also makes you realize you can do anything."

—JEFF MCCARTY

Nevertheless, getting a new, untested concept off the ground was brutal. McCarty had no real savings when he quit his job; in fact, he was $3,000 in debt. To support himself, he took freelance design jobs. One was a corporate identity redesign for Mozzi's Pizza, whose accomplished young owner, Mark Lee, McCarty looked to as a role model.

Lee spotted McCarty's time capsule and asked what it was. McCarty poured out his enthusiasm for the product—

and for the possibility of Lee's getting involved in his venture. Two hours later, they had agreed to become partners.

In 1991, Lee already had a chain of five pizza restaurants with combined sales of $2 million, so he knew he was capable of starting a successful business. But launching the time capsules was a whole new ballgame. "The pizza business is a cash business," Lee points out. "And you know how pizza is sold. With time capsules, we had to learn everything from scratch."

First they tried going directly to consumers, with magazine ads. Six months later, that strategy was an obvious bomb. The time capsules became more than just a money drain; they were a black hole. Lee had already invested twice what he had initially planned. Meanwhile, McCarty had racked up over $30,000 in personal debt, much of it financed by credit cards. "There were some very tense moments," Lee recalls.

But there was also a remarkable bond of consideration and respect between the partners, who had only been associates for a matter of months. Lee could see McCarty's connection with the product. And McCarty couldn't stand to fail Lee. "I was almost more worried about letting my partner down than I was about letting the business fail," says McCarty.

Whatever the motivation, it was a good thing they hung together. Their second marketing strategy hit pay dirt. They exhibited at a trade show for the health-care industry and attracted tons of interest from hospital gift shops. From there, they made a splash at gift shows and went on to sign a network of sales reps. Next came major retail accounts, appearances on QVC, and a raft of new products (including time capsule kits for brides and new graduates). The partners forecast sales of $2 million to $3 million by the end of 1998. And the new millennium will clearly be a landmark for the time capsule business. Already, The Original Time Capsule Company has a licensing agreement to produce a Times Square 2000 Time Capsule. Apparently, it isn't too soon to say "Cheers!"

Greg Brophy, 35

Shred-it America Inc.

WHAT THEY DO: Franchise a mobile
paper shredding service; 53 locations, primarily in the United
States and Canada

HOME BASE: Mississauga, Ontario

FOUNDED: 1989

START-UP COSTS: $192,000

1997 SALES: Over $43 million

1998 PROJECTIONS: Over $80 million

Photo Courtesy: Shred-it America Inc.

On a tip from his lawyer, Greg Brophy met with the owner of a "shredding truck" in Ottawa. Here was a guy driving from building to building, shredding documents on his truck for various companies. Not what you would call impressive. Not the kind of thing that would bowl over a 26-year-old who had already made a mint buying and renovating houses while going to college.

Piecing It Together

I It's not the business you're in, but the way you do business, that makes the difference. Every business has a formula for making money. You need the determination to figure out the formula for your particular business."

But Brophy kept an open mind. He knew that businesses were becoming increasingly concerned about security. And apparently, shredding documents yourself isn't always a piece of cake. "It's very wasteful," observes Brophy. "The shredder jams if there's a paper clip or staple put through, and it's dangerous for the employee using it." Besides, who wants to pay a salaried staffer good money to run the paper shredder?

"I started looking at ways to build up the concept—salespeople, security containers, telemarketing," recalls Brophy. When he was done, mobile paper shredding didn't seem like such a bad idea after all. Brophy's next move was to canvass businesses in Toronto to find out who might use the service. "Fifty-five of the people I talked to said they'd be interested," says Brophy. "I took my list to the bank and secured a loan."

He began with just one truck and shredder. "Within three weeks, we were so booked, I had to lease another truck," Brophy says.

The demand that made Shred-it America a booming business proved explosive in more ways than one. "When you grow like we did, you play catch-up for a long time," says Brophy. "I was running out of cash all the time, and I wasn't able to get financing as easily as I had hoped. Banks looked at me and saw this very enthusiastic person who hadn't done much [in the business world] yet."

After a year and a half, Brophy hired a consultant. "I met with him in his office and he advised me to liquidate," he says. "I remember going down the elevator from the seventh floor and feeling like my spirits were sinking with the elevator. But by the time I walked through the lobby and touched the front door, I had decided that, no, I wasn't going to quit. I wasn't going to give up. I knew that tenacity was the key in any small business.

"So I said, 'He's pointed out some weaknesses. I'm going to work on those. I can increase profitability. I can increase density at the roots. But I'm not giving up,'" Brophy recalls. "I guess I have a certain personality that doesn't like to quit."

It's a personality Brophy is glad for now—when Shred-it America is franchising by leaps and bounds and per-unit sales are expected to double this year. Sales for 1998 are projected to reach $80 million, certainly more than that consultant would have imagined possible. Brophy admits it's taken more than a little obsessiveness to bring the company to its current level—"There's not a lot of balance in life when you're starting a business," he reports—but he also says there is hope on that front. "Now, I work hard during the week, but I take time off on the weekend to enjoy my family."

He enjoys the business, too—knowing that it's on solid footing, and knowing what it took to get there. "I cannot believe how well life has turned out," Brophy says. "I walk in every day and say, 'This is cool.'"

Chapter 10

Get A Life

"Profits are like breathing.
You have to have them.
But who would stay alive
just to breathe?"

—MAURICE MASCARANHAS

Peter Caporilli, 35

Tidewater Workshop

WHAT THEY DO: Make and market
  cedar garden furniture and accessories
HOME BASE: Port Republic, New Jersey
FOUNDED: 1990
START-UP COSTS: $165
1997 SALES: Over $4.5 million
1998 PROJECTIONS: $7 million

Photo Courtesy: Tidewater Workshop

Peter Caporilli's childhood had the scent of cedar. He grew up around the family boat works, where rugged skiffs were formed from cedar planks. He smelled the wood and watched the hulls take shape. He learned woodworking, too. But it was a hopeless romance. By the time Caporilli was old enough to appreciate the beauty of the family business, the company his great-grandfather had launched at the turn of the century was already becoming a relic. Caporilli needed a future, and the future was not in wooden boats.

Still, his feeling for the family business ran deep. He went to college, then on to a career in marketing. While working for the Burpee Seed Co., Caporilli attracted the attention of John Burpee—not just for his good work, but for his woodworking ability. "He knew I did woodworking as a hobby, and he asked me to make a bench," recalls Caporilli. That bench became so celebrated among the Burpee staff that Caporilli soon found a part-time vocation making benches for co-workers and their friends.

Seaworthy

"There are so many rewards to having this business. Maybe the most important one is that I feel I have a responsibility to what I've been given and the opportunities I've had—and I feel like I've made the most of them."

Finally, someone suggested that Caporilli try advertising. The day his first newspaper ad ran, he took $1,500 in orders. In 1991, Caporilli left Burpee to establish Tidewater Workshop. He did a brief stint at the catalog company Hanover Direct after setting up shop, but quit early in 1992. "I missed the business too much," explains Caporilli.

Like his great-grandfather's boat works, Caporilli's concern is a family affair. His mother, father, sister and brother all hold executive positions. Even the tools have a history. "[Many] are what we used on the hulls of the boats we made," Caporilli reports.

Because of Caporilli's marketing savvy, Tidewater Workshop has never suffered from insufficient demand. On the contrary, he says, "We have never been able to keep up with it." Though the company could sell enough benches to justify the creation of a giant automated plant, Caporilli heartily rejects the notion. "At some point, we'd just be taking orders and never putting our hands on anything," he reasons. "When we send out a bench, we know that a lot of hands have touched it.

"I think the key to our success is that we've been able to identify a product that people have a relationship with, not only because of its inherent value as a bench but because of the way it's made."

Photo© Bruce Zake

Michael Krause, 19
Daniel Krause, 30
Kate Krause, 27

ExchangeNet

WHAT THEY DO: Provide Internet service
    to the Cleveland area
HOME BASE: Cleveland
FOUNDED: 1994
START-UP COSTS: $10,000
1997 SALES: Over $1 million
1998 PROJECTIONS: Over $2 million

Most teenagers are happy to flip hamburgers for mini-
mum wage. Not Michael Krause. At age 14, he solicited the
help of his brother Daniel and launched what is now
Cleveland's largest local Internet service provider, ExchangeNet.

"Starting the business was Michael's idea. He was into
computers and he had the foresight to know that this was
a good opportunity," says Daniel. "He approached me because he didn't have any money."

Daniel—who is 11 years older—observes that it isn't
easy to do business when you're 14. "At the beginning, I
spent a lot of time with my brother counseling him on how

Net Gain

"On the one hand, I look at companies [that
have gone public] like Mindspring and think,
'Why didn't we do that?' Grow the company, raise
money, take it public. At the same time, we're
getting 250 to 300 new accounts per month. We
have 8,000 clients, which is incredible. Last year,
we increased revenues by over 40 percent. And,
no, there has never been a time when we thought
we might have to close our doors. So by those
measures, I'm very happy with where we are."

—DANIEL KRAUSE

to deal with customer support, for example," Daniel recalls. "He approached it like a 14-year-old would. If he
didn't like someone's attitude, his inclination was not to
call him back."

At the same time, Michael sees some advantages to starting young. "Clients are impressed when they see [young people who] know what they're talking about," he contends.

Still, the miracle of this story is not that a smart teenager and his 25-year-old brother started a million-dollar business. It's that they did it while managing to live the lives of a 14- and 25-year-old.

Michael, for example, finished high school and went on to college at Cleveland State University, where he studies music—when he's not on the job as ExchangeNet's systems administrator. Daniel had—and still has—a career in financial services, selling investments. He is not involved in ExchangeNet's daily operations. But his wife, Kate, is. A part-owner, she took over the management of the company in 1995 and continues to run operations today.

The ExchangeNet partnership doesn't follow a typical pattern, probably because none of its principals expected to be running a million-dollar company so early in life. Daniel and Michael weren't pessimistic at the outset, but they didn't exactly anticipate the Internet boom of the past few years. "When we began, there was no such thing as World Wide Web mania," says Daniel. "We were doing dial-up text-based accounts, if anyone can remember what those are. We had no idea that the company would grow to be what it is today."

As for Kate, she was already pursuing a career in business after graduating from college. But moving to Cleveland and taking charge of what is now a 20-person staff wasn't what she foresaw, either.

Yet somehow the pieces fit. Michael has created a vocation that will complement a career in music, if that's what he chooses. Kate has authority and responsibility that might have taken decades to win in a traditional corporate environment. And Daniel has the benefits of a corporate career with the emotional payoff of business ownership.

Conventional wisdom may tell you that starting a business and having a life are incompatible. The Krauses will tell you it's not only possible, but necessary. A well-pitched business flies—and flies and flies. And meanwhile, life doesn't wait.

Vicki Morgan, 39

Foghorn Press Inc.

WHAT THEY DO: Publish books, primarily related to outdoor recreation and travel

HOME BASE: Petaluma, California

FOUNDED: 1985

START-UP COSTS: $25,000

1997 SALES: $1.4 million

1998 PROJECTIONS: $1.5 million

Vicki Morgan is sure she's supposed to be an entrepreneur. She knows it in her bones, where it counts. But she's still figuring out what it means to be an entrepreneur— what matters, what doesn't, and how to recognize success when the face of it keeps changing.

Her story begins with the usual spunk. She was a newspaper reporter in San Diego when she teamed up with a sports writer to self-publish a history of the San Francisco 49ers. Morgan used her credit cards to raise most of the $25,000 needed to finance the book. Thankfully, it was an instant success.

From there, Morgan parlayed a love of the outdoors into a series of regional recreation guides and travel books with nationwide appeal. The business grew and prospered. She hired a staff. She worked 80-hour weeks. She leased office space in San Francisco's trendy SoMa district. Morgan thought she had made it.

Got It In Writing

I have a Paul Hawken quote hanging in my office: 'Limits and prosperity are intimately linked.' I never really got that until last year, but now I know exactly what it means."

But then the priorities changed. "[In 1997,] I moved up to Sonoma County, where I'm from," she says. "I had begun to look at ways to incorporate more of my life into running the business." That process accelerated when Morgan was forced to take a few months off to deal with a serious illness. "What the illness did was underline the value of what I was trying to do," she says. "All of a sudden, I couldn't do the long commute. I couldn't work 60 or 80 hours a week." Even after she returned to work, she wasn't up to her usual workaholic pace.

Change was inevitable and, in many ways, painful. Morgan downsized the company, moved out of the San

Francisco office, decentralized operations, scaled back growth plans—in short, deconstructed much of what she had spent years building.

But in the midst of the chaos and exhaustion, there was hope. "It was the first year we posted a profit in three years," says Morgan. "I began working from home, and it's been great. My commute is up the stairs. I don't have to put on my power clothing. I have more flexibility on hours, less distraction." Now, the marketing and editorial departments work from Morgan's home office, while other departments are stationed elsewhere. "The separation of departments has made us more productive," says Morgan. "There was a high interaction factor before that didn't need to be there."

Morgan concedes that Foghorn Press no longer looks the part of a successful publishing house. She also observes that that no longer interests her. Success now is smaller, more private—and maybe more profound. "As you recreate yourself as an entrepreneur, you recreate your business," she says. "It's all part of your life experience. Business is just another metaphor for the journey. It's an exercise in knowing yourself."

Jennifer Barclay, 32

Blue Fish Clothing Co.

WHAT THEY DO: Design artisan-pro-
duced, natural-fiber, hand-block-
printed clothing; operate five
retail boutiques
HOME BASE: Frenchtown, New Jersey
FOUNDED: 1985
START-UP COSTS: Less than $100
1997 SALES: $13.8 million
1998 PROJECTIONS: Not available

Photo Courtesy: Blue Fish Clothing Co.

At 17, it was all about expression. The year was 1985, and Jennifer Barclay was hand-printing designs onto T-shirts in her parents' garage. She took them to a local fair and made $450, which represented better than a 450 percent markup.

She had the profit margin. And she had a style that won followers from the very first day. Barclay was—and still is—a visionary. And with attitude . . . the kind of attitude that comes from being 17 and idealistic and groovy and in demand.

She began making dresses and shirts printed with her trademark whimsical patterns and selling them at craft shows and jazz festivals. In 1986, she attended her first trade show in New York and took orders for 6,000 pieces. This was heady stuff.

Something Fishy

*"*It takes tremendous inner resources to change with your business, and definitely moments of self-doubt come. But I just try to gain clarity, prioritize what I have to do, make clear my intentions, and start bravely marching forward. When I started the business, it used to be a stubborn, immature 'I can do it!' Now, I know I can do it. It comes from a different place."

"I had no idea how to make 6,000 garments in four months," says Barclay. "My friends and I worked like crazy. We rolled out our sleeping bags in the middle of the workshop and worked around the clock, cutting and sewing and dyeing and block-printing." They made their deadline—and in doing so created a mythology that would help drive the business long after it took on a manufacturing facility and retail stores and celebrity clients and publicly traded stock.

Blue Fish is not—and has never been—an ordinary clothing company. In addition to its artistic mystique, this company has principles to uphold. It uses recycled, "reprocessed" and organically grown cotton. It insists on one-of-a-kind printing by hand to maintain its distinctive look. It sponsors a community outreach program, BlueFishgarten, to bring hands-on art workshops to schools and community groups.

Blue Fish is successful by any measure. Fans have become collectors, with an average of 35 to 50 pieces of Blue Fish clothing in their closets. Sales have grown astronomically each year. And the financial gains have a silver lining—they also help promote social and environmental consciousness.

Yet Barclay isn't finished—not by several yards. She is branching out in new design directions. "We're adding new fabrics—hemp silks and woven silk linens—and creating clothes that are more sophisticated," she says. "They'll be wearable to work or for special occasions."

Barclay is looking for a new sophistication in operations as well. "In the beginning, [the company] was about blatant creativity and being one big, happy family," she says. "We were a lot of young people who thought we could conquer the world—and we did. But now the challenges are different. We need to work together as a team in a way that makes sense, where members can really rely on each other."

Such changes in the fabric of Barclay's business are, in her words, "difficult and enlivening." It's tough, she says, "getting people to welcome change, to have the vision to see beyond today." On the other hand, it's part of the evanescence that makes Blue Fish interesting to consumers—and to stockholders, employees, admirers and even Barclay herself.

"It's been a constant process of personal growth," she says. "If you let it be scary, you can be pulled down by it. But it's also a tremendous opportunity."

Tracy Porter, 30
John Porter, 37

Stonehouse Farm Goods

WHAT THEY DO: License fanciful designs
  for furnishings and household
  goods
HOME BASE: Princeton, Wisconsin
FOUNDED: 1991
START-UP COSTS: $5,000
1997 SALES: $19 million
1998 PROJECTIONS: $30 million

In 1991, Tracy and John Porter dreamed of a beautiful life in the country. They envisioned sheep and horses, lots of land, and the kind of work they could pour their hearts into.

The Porters were like many young, urban couples—hip, successful, and strangely unfulfilled. They lived in Chicago, where both worked as fashion models. It was hardly a miserable existence, and yet they couldn't help feeling their lives lacked a certain—well, *life*.

So, with $5,000 they borrowed from family members, the Porters moved to Princeton, Wisconsin, and began making hand-painted furniture under the name Stonehouse Farm Goods. Though they shared an artistic flair, the notion of starting a furniture company was pure fancy. "Sometimes I think the reason we got into [making furniture] was that we wanted furniture like this for our home and couldn't afford to go to Marshall Field's to buy it," jokes Tracy. The Porters' original studio—a converted chicken coop—was so cold in the winter that they had to heat their paints under an electric blanket.

As Beautiful As You Make It

I think it's healthy to walk into things with your rose-colored glasses. If we had known how hard it would be to build this business, we might never have attempted it. A lot of people don't give themselves enough credit. You never know what your destiny will be until you try."

—TRACY PORTER

Their products, on the other hand, generated plenty of heat. At their first trade show in 1992, the Porters took in orders worth more than $75,000. Demand was so high that buyers did the inconceivable and prepaid for their orders.

Since then, Stonehouse Farm Goods has grown, and grown up. By 1995, sales had topped $8 million, but managing the company's manufacturing operations was becoming unwieldy. "We started evaluating," says Tracy. "We asked, 'What are our strengths? What do we really want to do?' And we decided to [switch to] licensing our designs." Now, 20 manufacturers—many of them industry leaders—produce goods for their product line, Tracy Porter—The Home Collection. Items range from carpets to dinnerware and bath fixtures. In 1997, combined retail sales of goods for the label reached $19 million. Sales in 1998 are projected to hit $30 million. Not bad for a simple country business.

And not bad for the Porters, either. Running a multimillion-dollar company isn't exactly stress-free. "We definitely have days when we feel we're succeeding in spite of ourselves," says Tracy. Yet she also notes that the pursuit of happiness has been a noble and worthwhile goal.

"We have this really cool group of people who all love being here," she says. "We're really lucky to have each other; together, we have this awesome mind meld. It feels like we can do anything." In fact, considering that a staff of just nine creates the scores of designs that make up the Tracy Porter line, the productivity level is near miraculous.

So is the satisfaction level. "I loved the city, but I get so wired there that I think I'm less productive," Tracy reflects. "[Life here] is simpler. It's nice. Our studio is on the property where we live; it's a minute and a half walk to work. We get in the house at a really normal hour."

A successful business that thrives in tandem with an idyllic life? Apparently, it's not impossible. "Rather than selling just the products, we sell the romance of what we've done, the lifestyle we've created here," says John. "People tell us we're living the American dream." At the very least, they're living their own.

1.

Improve your business.

2.

See the latest trends.

3.

Download free/trial software.

4.

Learn to increase income.

5.

Find your dream business.

6.

Network with your peers.

FREE ADVICE

When was the last time you got *free* advice that was worth something?

Entrepreneur Magazine, the leading small business authority, is loaded with free advice—advice that could be worth millions to you. Every issue gives you detailed, practical knowledge on how to start a business and run it successfully. Entrepreneur is the perfect resource to keep small business owners up-to-date, on track, and growing their business.

BREAK OUT

Business Start-Ups helps you **break** out of the 9–5 life!

Do you want to get out of the 9–5 routine and take control of your life? Business Start-Ups shows you the franchise and business opportunities that will give you the future you dream of. Every issue answers your questions, highlights hot trends, spotlights new ideas, and provides the inspiration and real-life information you need to succeed.

MILLION DOLLAR SECRETS

free issue!

Exercise your right to make it **big.**

Get into the small business authority—
now at **80% off** the newsstand price!

Yes! Start my one year subscription and
bill me for just $9.99. I get a full year of Entrepreneur
and save 80% off the newsstand rate. If I choose not
to subscribe, the free issue is mine to keep.

Name ☐ Mr. ☐ Mrs. _____
(please print)

Address _____

City_____ State _____ Zip_____

☐ BILL ME ☐ PAYMENT ENCLOSED

Mail this coupon to **Entrepreneur** MAGAZINE. P.O. Box 50368, Boulder, CO 80321-0368

OPPORTUNITY KNOCKS!!!

free issue!

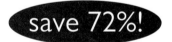

save 72%!

Please enter my subscription to Business
Start-Ups for one year. I will receive 12 issues for
only $9.99. That's a savings of 72% off the newsstand
price. The free issue is mine to keep, even if I choose
not to subscribe.

Name ☐ Mr. ☐ Mrs. _____
(please print)

Address _____

City_____ State _____ Zip_____

☐ BILL ME ☐ PAYMENT ENCLOSED

Mail this coupon to **Business Start-Ups** P.O. Box 50347, Boulder, CO 80321-0347

Entrepreneur Magazine's
SMALL BUSINESS EXPO®

Small Business Success Starts Here

Whether you're looking for a great new business idea or ways to help your existing business run better and grow faster, Entrepreneur Magazine's Small Business Expo is the place to be.

New Franchises & Business Opportunities
The Latest Business Products & Services

FREE SEMINARS:

Writing a Business Plan • Raising Capital
Operating a Homebased Business
Growing Your Business • Sales & Marketing
AND MORE!